Where to
wager in
Illinois, Iowa,
Minnesota,
North Dakota,
South Dakota
and Wisconsin

GUIDE TO
Midwest
Casinos

By David Hawley

Andrews and McMeel
A Universal Press Syndicate Company
Kansas City

Pioneer Books are published for the St. Paul Pioneer Press by Andrews and McMeel. Additional copies may be ordered by calling (800) 642-6480.

Library of Congress Cataloging-in-Publication Data

Hawley, David, 1946–
    Guide to Midwest casinos : where to wager in Illinois, Iowa, Minnesota, North Dakota, South Dakota, and Wisconsin / by David Hawley.
        p.   cm. — (Pioneer books)
    ISBN 0-8362-8081-4 : $8.95
    1. Casinos—Middle West—Guidebooks. 2. Gambling—Middle West—Guidebooks. I. Title. II. Series: Pioneer books (Kansas City, Mo.)
    HV6721.M54H39   1994
    338.7′61795′02577—dc20   94-17505
                                                                                                           CIP

PIONEER 🏛 BOOKS

Editor: Sam Elrod
Editorial Director: David A. Fryxell
Promotion Director: Chris Oshikata
Design Director: Larry May
Cover Design: Larry May
Cover Photo: Bill Alkofer
Maps and illustrations: David Hardman

Contents

Chapter 1: Introduction

Chapter 2: Illinois

Chapter 3: Iowa

Chapter 4: Minnesota

Chapter 5: North Dakota

Chapter 6: South Dakota

Chapter 7: Wisconsin

Chapter 8: Playing the Games

About the Author

CHAPTER 1

INTRODUCTION

The Midwest Gambling Scene

This is a guide to casinos in America's heartland, which means it's also a book about traveling.

Not that long ago, visiting a casino for a Midwesterner meant a trip to Nevada or New Jersey. That has changed in one respect—you don't have to travel as far.

But most people still have to log some distance to reach their nearest gambling hall because many casinos in the Midwest are in out-of-the-way places, such as Indian reservations or formerly distressed riverfront areas. And who wants to visit just one? There are more than 120 casinos in the six states covered by this guide, but except for those in Deadwood, S.D., few are close to each other.

We started with the presumption that people do more in a casino than gamble. As seekers of entertainment, casino patrons also are interested in what casinos look like, what amenities they offer, and if it's possible to get any "deals," such as coupons, discounted motel rooms, or casino club perks. They also want to know what the area is like near the casino and if there's anything to do there besides gamble. And they'd like some information about hotels and resorts.

This guide covers all this in the style of a consumer's handbook, organized for browsing state-by-state. For each casino, we describe the facility, list the games and unique rules for playing them, and include information about hours of operation, food and liquor services, hotels, area attractions and other amenities. And for first-time gamblers, we've also included some basic tips on playing the games, plus some advice on good, in-depth books about blackjack, video poker and craps.

When it comes to casinos, the old adage, "seen one, seen 'em all," simply isn't true. For example, all the casinos in Illinois and most of the casinos in Iowa are on riverboats—some big and lavish, some tiny and cramped. Most people play blackjack or slots at South Dakota casinos, but if you want to play video poker, look elsewhere. North Dakota has only four casinos of any size, but you can play blackjack in more than 300 locations. Minnesota has the biggest casinos in the region, but many of them don't serve alcoholic beverages and offer child care instead. Some casinos are part of resort complexes, while others stand alone in the middle of the woods. Casino food is a big subject in Minnesota, not so big in Wisconsin. And Deadwood, S.D., has more than 60 mini-casinos, most located on both sides of one historic Old West street.

Visiting all the casinos in six states required nearly 9,000 miles of traveling, mostly by car. Some casinos, especially those in Iowa and Illinois, were in large cities. Some of the casinos in other states were located in places that gave new meaning to the expression, "in the middle of nowhere."

But all had one thing in common: They had lots of customers. Between 1990 and 1993, three of the states in this guide—Minnesota, Wisconsin and Illinois—moved into the top 10 gambling "feeder states" in the nation, according to a study conducted by Harrah's. The gaming industry refers to "feeders" as areas that generate large numbers of visits to casinos.

The Midwest also made Harrah's top-10 list of cities that generated the most visits to casinos in 1993. The list included Minneapolis/St. Paul, Chicago, Milwaukee and Green Bay.

The explosive growth of gambling in the Midwest posed the single most difficult challenge in creating this guide. Everything changes—and changes fast. It is rare to find a casino that doesn't have an expansion plan. At this point, most are getting ready for Phase 3, Phase 4 or Phase 5.

In Iowa, legislative action in 1994 that eliminated betting limits and restrictions on riverboats was expected to fuel an explosive growth spurt in the gaming industry. In Illinois, meanwhile, an effort to allow riverboats in downtown Chicago prompted nervous nail-biting among the operators of the huge riverboat casinos in Chicago's ring cities.

Take this guide with you on your next vacation, or use it to plan ahead. But be prepared for surprises. And, as they say over and over at every casino, good luck.

—David Hawley

CHAPTER 2
ILLINOIS

The Rules of the Game: To go to a casino in Illinois, you have to get on a riverboat. While this may seem like a romantic adventure to some, many gamblers hate being confined on a boat and dislike the restrictions imposed by boarding procedures.

For others, a cruise on a riverboat casino is a terrific experience. Most of the boats have a variety of amenities, and a few are downright opulent. To those who like to jostle around the tables and hear the roar of approval at a hot throw of the dice, a riverboat is the place to be. And if you like to sit out on a deck and watch the world go by, you'll have plenty of opportunity for that—since the non-gambling areas of most boats are virtually deserted.

A gambling cruise usually lasts from two to three hours. Typically, you have 30 minutes to board the boat before the cruise begins and you can remain on board, and gamble, for 30 minutes after the boat returns to the dock. The boat cruises for one to two hours.

Under Illinois law, boarding a riverboat is restricted to the 30-minute period before the cruise begins. In winter or during bad weather, the boat may never leave the dock—but you still can't get on after the boarding period. And if you get off at any time during the session, you can't get back on until the next session begins.

Of course, if the boat is cruising, you have to stay on until it returns to the dock. If you've made a tidy profit at the tables or the slot machines, the temptation is great to keep gambling until the end of the cruise. For this reason, riding a casino boat sometimes poses the kind of dilemma that Pinocchio faced when he visited Pleasure Island: He knew that if he stayed, he'd probably be turned into an ass.

For some, the gambling cruise is either too short or too long. And while ticket prices have been dramatically slashed since the launching of the first Illinois riverboat in 1991, a lot of people hate the idea of paying admission to a casino—even if the ticket costs less than a bet on one hand of blackjack.

Until 1994, the boarding rules for Illinois and Iowa were virtually identical. But Iowa dumped its boarding restrictions in April, allowing customers to board boats whenever they are docked. Illinois is expected to follow suit.

For casino operators, running a riverboat is no picnic. The investment is huge—just applying for a license includes a $50,000 fee—and maintaining a boat is incredibly expensive. Riverboat casinos need lots of passengers who bring lots of money.

Nonetheless, riverboat gambling in Illinois has been a rousing success. Back in 1991, the legislature authorized the granting of up to 10 riverboat casino licenses. With the opening of the Grand Victoria Riverboat in Elgin in the fall of 1994, all 10 casinos will be operating, three of them with more than one boat. The law permits up to two boats under each license.

Riverboat gambling was legalized for the purpose of pumping new life into depressed riverfront areas and to promote tourism. Chicago was excluded from riverboat development and politicians are currently trying to coax state legislators into amending the law to permit up to six boats on the Chicago River.

Illinois riverboats offer slots, video games, blackjack, craps, roulette, baccarat and Big Six money wheels. There are no limits, either on betting or overall loses. Most casinos won't permit bets in excess of $2,000 on any table, but the management has the option of eliminating limits for certain privileged players.

Casino operators are required to report the average payout on slot machines and many use payout statistics in their advertising. Early in 1994, the casinos were reporting average slot payouts of between 91 and 96 percent.

All of the boats are set up the same way. You enter a pavilion, where you buy your tickets. For evening sessions, it's often wise to reserve the tickets in advance.

The pavilions have bars, restaurants, gift shops, snack bars and maybe even live entertainment. Some, like the Hollywood Casino's Art Deco pavilion in Aurora, Ill., are incredibly elaborate. If you're making a evening of it, you dine on shore; the only Illinois riverboat big enough to have a full-sized on-board restaurant is the *Casino Queen* in East St. Louis.

As the time to board nears, crowds begin forming at the boarding ramp. Slot-playing regulars usually come early and wait at the front of the line, ready to be first at their favorite machines. When the gate opens, there's a mad push, though guards are careful to keep track of every guest. The casino has to pay the state a $2 tax for each patron.

Aboard, the gaming areas can range from not-too-crowded to so crowded

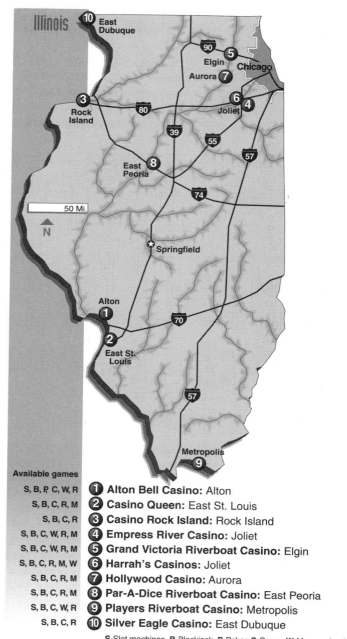

Illinois

East Dubuque

Elgin

Chicago

Aurora

Rock Island

Joliet

East Peoria

50 Mi.

N

Springfield

Alton

East St. Louis

Metropolis

Available games

Games		Casino	Location
S, B, P, C, W, R	❶	**Alton Bell Casino:**	Alton
S, B, C, R, M	❷	**Casino Queen:**	East St. Louis
S, B, C, R	❸	**Casino Rock Island:**	Rock Island
S, B, C, W, R, M	❹	**Empress River Casino:**	Joliet
S, B, C, W, R, M	❺	**Grand Victoria Riverboat Casino:**	Elgin
S, B, C, R, M, W	❻	**Harrah's Casinos:**	Joliet
S, B, C, R, M	❼	**Hollywood Casino:**	Aurora
S, B, C, R, M	❽	**Par-A-Dice Riverboat Casino:**	East Peoria
S, B, C, W, R	❾	**Players Riverboat Casino:**	Metropolis
S, B, C, R	❿	**Silver Eagle Casino:**	East Dubuque

S-Slot machines, **B**-Blackjack, **P**-Poker, **C**-Craps, **W**-Money wheel, **R**-Roulette, **M**-Mini-Baccarat that you can faint and not fall down. Things have improved in recent years; most riverboats now limit the number of passengers to about three-fourths of the total number that can legally board.

On some boats, you won't know when your voyage is underway. Others have plenty of windows and the nineteenth-century, Mark Twain–type replicas have open decks on each level. Aside from the hum of the engines and a mild vibration of the decks, you won't notice anything unusual. Being on a riverboat casino is like visiting most dry-land gambling joints—just a bit cozier.

The Name of the Game: With the exception of the far eastern parts of the state, Illinois is nicely sprinkled with riverboat casinos. Chicago is ringed by riverboats in Elgin, Aurora and Joliet, all within an hour of the city. Northwest Illinois has a riverboat in East Dubuque, and the Mississippi along the border with Iowa and Missouri has casinos in Rock Island, Alton and East St. Louis. In the far, far south is a casino in Metropolis, just across the river from Paducah, Ky. Central Illinois has a casino in East Peoria.

All of the casinos appear to be thriving, though Illinois riverboat operators are nervously awaiting the start of a riverboat casino industry in Missouri and they are troubled by moves to eliminate betting limits in Iowa. And, they say, the whole game will change if riverboat gambling ever comes to downtown Chicago.

Alton Belle Casino II
....

Alton, Illinois
800-336-7568

Getting There: From Illinois, take Highway 140 from Interstate 55 or Highway 143 from Interstate 70. When you reach Alton, take Highway 67 to the river. From Missouri, take Highway 67 across the new Clark Bridge, then follow the signs.

First Impression: Little Caesar's Palace.

Overview: Alton is one of the many fine old river towns that were damaged by the 1993 flood of the Mississippi River. Fortunately, most of the town is on a steep riverbank and was spared. However, the flood coincided with the launching in May of the new *Alton Belle II*, a beamy, cruise-type boat. The boat survived, but the plan to market it as an upscale luxury casino with a Roman theme had to be modified. Cruise prices, which once ranged as high as $20, were slashed, and the boat now specializes in quick-turnover cruises that include one hour on the river and an additional hour dockside.

There's plenty of parking in the narrow flats downriver from the *Alton Belle* pavilion, though most visitors hop a shuttle bus after parking their cars. The three-story pavilion appears promising from the outside, but the first two levels are something of a disappointment—looking like the concession area at a ballpark. The third level is much nicer; it has two restaurants—Belle's Buffet and an upscale steak house called Victors—plus a big sports bar called Aces, where bands and stage acts are featured.

The Boat: The *Alton Belle II* is a 222-foot boat that has a wide, 66-foot beam. The broad gaming areas on the first two decks stretch from hull to hull. The third level has a pleasant three-quarter aft sun deck and there's a topside outdoor deck that's not handicapped accessible. A boat this beamy requires the support of interior stanchions, which are covered with Ionic capitals at the ceiling—sort of a Roman ruin in reverse. There's a lot of black marble throughout the boat, but the most striking feature is a series of hand-carved glass panels in the stairwell that depict old Roman coins and architectural ruins. All in all, it's a handsome place.

The Casino: It may be big, but you know you're on a boat when you ride the *Alton Belle*. The gaming areas are overcrowded with slot machines that are set in narrow aisles. They're also noisy places, though a small area has been set aside on the third deck for a deli lounge. The boat has two bars, with the typical built-in poker machines. The cruise is short, so the action tends to be intense. The *Belle* also does heavy business with tour groups, offering a bewildering variety of packages. If you're not with a group, you know it.

Cruises: Eight daily, plus an extra red-eye cruise on Fridays and Saturdays. Each cruise lasts for one hour, with a two-hour gaming session. Admission $4, or $3 for seniors.

In Play: 650 slot and video games (video poker, keno), quarter to $5 machines. 32 blackjack tables ($5–unlimited), using six-deck shoes (four splits allowed, with double downs after splits except for aces, which require one additional card). Big Six Wheel. Four craps tables ($5–$500), paying double odds and using standard Las Vegas layout. Three roulette tables, ($10 anyway, $15 outside). Two Caribbean stud poker tables ($5–$500).

Specials: Card club. Rated players admitted to Argosy VIP lounge at the pavilion.

Amenities: Two bars and deli on boat. Restaurant and buffet dining at the pavilion, plus a bar with an entertainment area.

Overnight: Cruise/hotel packages that include cruise tickets, a casino meal, coupon book and boarding ticket are offered at 10 hotels in the Alton area. Some of the hotels also include a continental breakfast with the package. The participating hotels are: Holiday Inn–Alton, $38 with breakfast (618-462-1220); Holiday Inn–St. Louis, $45 (314-621-8200); Ramada Inn–

Alton, $28 (618-463-0800); Drury Inn in St. Ann, Mo., $43 including breakfast and round-trip transportation to casino (314-429-2255); Best Western–Collinsville, $29 including breakfast (618-345-5660); Quality Inn– Collinsville, $27.50 including breakfast (618-344-7171); Pere Marquette Lodge in Grafton, $44 including breakfast (618-786-2331); Stouffer Concourse Hotel in St. Louis, $44.50 including breakfast (314-429-1100); Marriott Pavilion in St. Louis, $35 including breakfast (314-421-1776); and Best Western Airport Inn in St. Louis, $37.50 including breakfast (314-427-5955).

Other Reasons to Be Here: Alton has a reputation for antique shops and cafes. Some 50 shops are within walking distance from the casino, though the hilly bluffs will make your legs ache. But many of the antique stores double as cafes, providing plenty of opportunities to rest. Other attractions include the Raging Rivers Water Park, a number of golf courses, Pere Marquette State Park and the Gordon Moore Park. For more information, call the Alton Convention and Visitors Bureau, 800-258-6645.

Casino Queen

East St. Louis, Illinois
800-993-2724
618-874-5000

Getting There: From Illinois, take Interstate 55 and exit at Fourth Street, then follow the signs. From Missouri, take Interstate 70, exit at Third Street and follow the signs.

First Impression: Ahhh, no claustrophobia.

Overview: East St. Louis has the reputation of being one of the poorest and most violent cities in the nation. People don't come to this side of the river for sightseeing, but they do come here to gamble. The pavilion berth for the *Casino Queen* was placed just south of the I-70/I-55 interchange so that customers won't have trouble finding it. Once you exit the expressway, you follow light-pole signs that are placed about every 50 feet, leading you past the rubble of broken-up buildings to the new riverfront developments. The pavilion has a 15-acre, well-guarded parking lot—and it's free. In 1994, the St. Louis light-rail system, called Metrolink, opened a terminal for the *Casino Queen*, making it possible to ride from the airport and down-town St. Louis to the casino's parking lot.

The casino's brick-and-glass pavilion is enormous, feeling like an air-line terminal. The pavilion has a long bar along the windowless riverside wall, plus a gift shop, snack bar and coat check. You can also sign up for the free slot club before you board; bonus points get you merchandise ranging from free breakfasts to admission tickets to the Six Flags amusement park near St. Louis.

The Boat: When she was launched in 1993, the *Casino Queen* became the largest inland vessel in America, though it lost that honor when the *Grand Victoria* was launched in Elgin late in 1994. Built to look like a classic sidewheeler, the *Casino Queen* is 460 feet long and has a beam of 70 feet. The boat is big enough to have a three-level atrium walkway in the bow, complete with chandelier, and each of her three gaming decks is divided into spacious fore and aft salons. A canopied lounge extends nearly the entire length of the fourth-level observation deck, where the views are glorious.

The Casino: Table games are emphasized on the *Casino Queen*, though the boat is big enough to accommodate more than 900 slot and video machines. Each of the three gaming decks has a bar, and the aft salon of the second deck is a huge buffet restaurant. Plans to include an additional fine-dining restaurant were scuttled in favor of additional gaming space. For all its spaciousness, the *Casino Queen* is primarily a gambling ship. Live entertainment on board is rare and so are gambling tournaments, which tend to take up space. On the other hand, strolling about the solid-feeling boat is a pleasure, especially on balmy days.

Cruises: Seven daily, each three-hour gaming sessions with up to two hours cruising. Admission: $2 to $5.

In Play: 906 slot and video games (video poker, keno), quarter to $5 machines. 46 blackjack tables ($2–$2,000), using six-deck shoes (dealer hits on soft 17s, double downs permitted after splitting, with exception of split aces, which require one additional card). 10 craps tables ($5–$2,000), using standard Las Vegas layout. Four roulette tables ($5–$2,000, total). Two mini-baccarat tables ($5–$2,000).

Specials: Slot club. Rated play. Some early cruise/breakfast specials.

Amenities: Liquor ($1.50 bar-brand drinks) on every deck. Entertainment at the visitor's pavilion. Buffet served aboard the boat. Deli and ice-cream parlor.

Overnight: The *Casino Queen* offers cruise/motel packages with many of the hotels in the St. Louis area, including the Embassy Suites, the Regal Hotel, and others. Call the casino for information.

Other Reasons to Be Here: All of St. Louis awaits you, including the famous Gateway Arch, the renowned zoo and Art Institute, Busch Stadium, tours of the Anheuser-Busch Brewery and the St. Louis Science Center, to name a few. And, by the way, St. Louis also is home to the Bowling Hall of Fame.

Casino Rock Island

Rock Island, Illinois
800-477-7747

Getting There: From Interstate 280, take Highway 92 to the Centennial Bridge. The Casino Rock Island staging area is in The Boatworks, just off Highway 92.

First Impression: Lotta boats.

Overview: Rock Island is part of a metro area called the Quad Cities, along with Moline in Illinois and Davenport and Bettendorf across the Mississippi River in Iowa. *Casino Rock Island* docks directly across the river from the mammoth *President Casino* in Davenport, and the two casinos appear to have successfully developed niche markets in their respective states. Davenport's *President* is a crowd-pleasing tourist boat, while *Casino Rock Island* pampers an upscale gambling clientele. The Illinois boat is the centerpiece in a four-vessel complex called The Boatworks. The largest of the boats is the *Ockerson*, a retrofitted dredge that serves as a ticketing barge, souvenir shop and a riverboat museum. Moored next to it is a former towboat that contains a 135-seat novelty bistro, where patrons sit amid the ship's exposed machinery. A third boat, a former tug, is used for casino offices.

The Boat: *The Casino Rock Island* is a 1991 working replica of a paddlewheel steamer (length, 214 feet; beam, 54 feet). It was built by hotelier Jim Jumer, who specializes in erecting elaborate European castles on the Midwestern plains. The boat is outfitted with custom oak and burl walnut woodwork that was fashioned in Jumer's woodworking shop in Peoria, plus antiques acquired in Europe. Acid-etched glass panels divide the main-deck gaming area from the bar and a comfortable bow lounge. The casino rooms glow in the light of hand-blown ruby lamps and there's lots of brocade drapery and flocked wallpaper.

Carefully arranged hors d'oeuvre buffets are located on each of the three decks; the food is free, while call-brand drinks cost just $1. The third deck has a small cabaret, usually reserved for folk artists. The boat can carry 1,000 passengers, but the usual limit is about 800, since the gaming area is less than 9,000 square feet.

The Casino: A refined atmosphere prevails here, despite the clatter of 400 slot machines. The games are typical for Illinois, with the exception of a group of machines called The District Slot Parlor that offer additional certificates good for merchandise or services at local shops or night clubs. A measure of the tone is revealed by the Paddlewheel Club, which is different from most card clubs because it requires minimum average wagers in order to be rated in one of four levels. To reach the Gold Card level, you have to wager an average of $100 per hand or cycle at least $1,000 through the slot machines on each cruise.

Cruises: Seven per day. The 10 A.M. and 7 P.M. cruises last two-and-a-half hours. Cruises at 8 A.M., 1, 3, 5, and 10 P.M. are one-and-a-half-hour cruises. Boarding is 15 minutes before departure. Admission is $4 to $10.

In Play: 400 slot and video games (video poker), quarter to $5 machines. 18 blackjack tables ($2–$2,000), using four- and six-deck shoes (dealer hits on soft 17s). Four craps tables ($2–$2,000). Two roulette tables ($2–$2,000).

Amenities: Complimentary hors d'oeuvres and low-priced ($1) drinks. Small restaurant at Boatworks staging area. Parking costs $3–$4. The Boatworks sponsors music festivals in the summer and the casino occasionally brings in headliner entertainers at local theaters.

Overnight: The casino offers a package with Jumer's Castle Lodge in Bettendorf that includes lodging, a prime rib dinner, transportation to the casino and boarding passes ($124–$133 for two); regular room rates are $83–$138 (319-359-7141). The Quad Cities Convention and Visitors Bureau publishes a list of more than 50 hotels and bed-and-breakfasts in the area (800-747-7800).

Other Reasons to Be Here: If two riverboat casinos aren't enough, you can visit Quad City Downs horse track in East Moline between April and October (309-792-0202). There's also the Fejervary Park Zoo in Davenport (319-326-7812) or the Niabi Zoo in Coal Valley, Ill., (309-799-5107) or the rose gardens at Vander Veer Conservatory in Davenport (319-326-7818). Wacky Waters in Davenport (319-388-9910) is the area's largest water park, with four water slides, power boats, dune buggies and a swimming beach. For the history-minded, there's the Colonel Davenport House in Rock Island (309-786-7336), the oldest home in the Quad Cities.

Empress River Casino

Joliet, Illinois
708-345-6789

Getting There: If traveling east on Interstate 80, take Exit 127, then turn south on Highway 6 and follow signs to the casino. If traveling west on I-80, take Exit 130A to Highway 7, turn right on Highway 6 and follow signs to the casino.

First Impression: Big crowds, big money.

Overview: You can visit the two big Empress boats without seeing much of Joliet. It's a big, industrial, working-class city that once housed Chicago gangsters in its state prison. The two Empress boats dock on the Des Plaines River in the southern suburbs of the city. Less than an hour's drive from downtown Chicago, the Empress tends to be the place patronized by high-rollers. Big money is wagered at the craps and roulette tables, and the atmosphere aboard is clogged with smoke and charged with excitement. Overcrowding was a major problem for the casino until a second, larger boat was added in 1993. In 1994, the casino expanded its pavilion, adding a 500-seat banquet facility, two full-service restaurants and two bars. You still pay $2 for parking, unless you hold the casino's free Platinum Club card; get one on your first visit.

The Boat: *The Empress I* (length 222 feet, beam 67 feet) and *Empress II* (length 238 feet, beam 67 feet) are sleek, high-powered cruise boats that barely vibrate while running with open throttles on the Des Plaines River. The newer of the boats, the *Empress II*, is 16 feet longer than her sister ship and has an enclosed third deck that houses a bar, deli and entertainment venue.

The Casino: Each boat has gaming areas on two decks, with very few windows and little room to walk around. Casino officials claim that complaints about poor ventilation on the *Empress I* have been addressed by establishing no-smoking tables on both boats. *Empress II* is considered the more gracious of the two boats, but serious gamblers tend to favor the all-business atmosphere on *Empress I*. The larger boat has a few more slot machines than her sister and three roulette wheels, compared to two wheels on *Empress I*. Many visitors to the Empress are content to plunk the quarter slots or play video poker in a relatively quiet bow area. But table players should expect to rub shoulders with experienced gamblers. At night, the atmosphere on these boats is loud and boisterous.

Cruises: 14 daily, each lasting two hours and 15 minutes, plus dockside gambling time. Admission: $2 to $10.

In Play: (each boat): Approximately 500 slot and video games (video poker, keno), quarter to $100 machines. 24 blackjack tables ($5–unlimited), using six-deck shoes (four splits allowed, double downs after splits permitted, except split aces, which require one additional card). Big Six Wheel. Four craps tables ($5–unlimited), paying double odds and using a standard Las Vegas layout. Two roulette tables (three tables on *Empress II*) ($3–unlimited). One mini-baccarat table ($10–unlimited).

Specials: Blackjack tournaments inaugurated in 1994.

Amenities: Liquor ($1.50) served in gaming areas. Live entertainment on weekends on *Empress II*. Dining and buffet services at the pavilion. Gift shop at pavilion. Special boarding and lounge services for rated players.

Overnight: The Holiday Inn–Joliet offers a special casino package for $89 that includes a room for two, cruise tickets and transportation to the casino (815-729-2000). Other lodging: The Red Roof Inn, $47 for two (815-741-2304).

Other Reasons to Be Here: The elegantly restored Rialto Square Theater at 102 N. Chicago St. offers big-name entertainment (815-726-6600). Also worth visiting is the Michigan Canal Museum Complex in Lockport, about 10 miles north of Joliet.

Grand Victoria Riverboat Casino

Elgin, Illinois

Getting There: Elgin is about 40 miles northwest of Chicago, off Interstate 90.

Overview: *The Grand Victoria* is scheduled to open late in 1994. The major partner in the venture is Hyatt Development Corp., a subsidiary of the hotel firm, which also operates a casino at Lake Tahoe and several casinos in the Caribbean. Plans call for a pavilion that will have two restaurants, a major bar and entertainment venue, plus a parking ramp for 1,400 vehicles.

The Boat: *The Grand Victoria* is expected to take the prize for the largest inland passenger vessel in America. Built at a cost of $30 million, the boat is 400 feet long and its beam is an astonishing 100 feet. The main deck has 30,000 square feet of gaming area, and the second-deck mezzanine has 6,000 square feet of gaming. The boat is designed to look like a nineteenth-century sidewheeler.

Cruises: Three-hour gambling sessions are planned, probably with two-hour cruising times.

In Play: Expect a big assortment of the casino games that are legal in Illinois: slots, video games, craps, roulette, blackjack and at least one Big Six Wheel. Mini-baccarat is under consideration.

Harrah's Casinos

Joliet, Illinois
800-427-7247

Getting There: From Chicago, take Interstate 55 to Exit 267 and turn left on Highway 53 to Ruby Street; turn left on Ruby Street, cross over the bridge and drive five blocks to Cass Street; turn right and continue to the casino. From the west or east, take Interstate 80 to Exit 131 (Center Street) and turn right on Jefferson Street. Cross the bridge, turn left on Joliet Street and continue to the casino. City routes to the casino are well-marked.

First Impression: Hurrah for the pirate king.

Overview: Joliet already had the *Empress Casino*, then the state's most successful riverboat, when Harrah's decided in 1993 to crash the riverboat market. The Nevada mega-casino corporation launched *Harrah's Northern Star* in May 1993 and added a second boat, *Harrah's Southern Star*, early in 1994. Both boats operate in downtown Joliet, using a 220-foot boat basin on the Des Plaines River that was constructed by the city. The Joliet section of the river is kept open throughout the year and both boats must cruise, since they share the same boarding ramp. Cruises are scheduled every 90 minutes.

Driving to the casino requires a ride through an older residential section, right into downtown. The casino has a 700-space parking ramp, which is free to cruise customers, plus another 250 spaces for valet parking. The pavilion is a brick and concrete building with a vast central hall under a three-story atrium tower. It houses the ticketing facilities and gift shop, plus a small Italian restaurant called Andreotti's, a deli and ice cream shop and two lounges, one with live entertainment. On crowded days (and most days are crowded), the pavilion is very loud. Harrah's has adopted a pirate theme and costumed buccaneers can be found roaming the pavilion, stirring up enthusiasm.

The Boats: Harrah's two boats are not identical. The *Northern Star* is a modern mega-yacht (length, 210 feet; beam, 67 feet). Its most striking feature is an open, three-deck casino atrium with its own glass-sided elevator. The *Southern Star*, by contrast, is a three-deck replica of a nineteenth-century sternwheeler that has larger dimensions (length, 210 feet; beam 77 feet), but a smaller capacity because of outside deck space. Both boats have non-smoking decks and high-stakes lounges, plus limited food services.

The Casinos: Harrah's has a reputation for service-oriented operations, and the Joliet boats meet those standards. Both are comfortable boats, with a mixture of quiet areas and loud, boisterous sections. The table games are handled with uniform precision. Tourists are welcomed; gamblers are even more welcomed. The casinos have a lot of quarter slot and video games for the low-investment player, but the table games require deeper pockets.

Cruises: 12 daily, starting at 8:30 A.M., plus an additional red-eye cruise on Fridays, Saturdays and holidays. Admission: $4 to $15.

In Play: Blackjack on both boats is played at $5–$2,000 tables, using six-deck shoes (splits to four hands are permitted, with double downs for all except split aces, which receive one additional card). Craps is $5–$2,000, with double odds and using a standard Las Vegas layout. Roulette is $5–$2,000. Mini-baccarat is $5–$2,000, with a 5 percent commission on house bets.

Northern Star: 570 slot games, quarter to one $100 machine. 77 video poker, video blackjack and video keno games, quarter to one $25 machine. 20 blackjack tables, two multiple-action blackjack tables. Five craps tables. Three roulette tables, one mini-baccarat table.

Southern Star: 365 slot games, quarter to one $100 machine. 53 video poker, video blackjack and video keno games, quarter to one $5 machine. 20 blackjack tables, two multiple-action blackjack tables. Four craps tables. Three roulette tables. One mini-baccarat table. One Big Six Wheel.

Amenities: Restaurants and bars at the Pavilion, including live entertainment every day and evening. Harrah's frequently books headliner stage shows at the Rialto Square Theatre, a refurbished vaudeville house about two blocks from the casino. Joining the Gold Card Club begins tracked play, resulting in complimentaries based on the discretion of the management. Gold Card members visiting any of the other Harrah's casinos get two free tickets to shows offered at those facilities. The card also is good for a 10 percent discount on gift-shop merchandise.

Overnight: Harrah's has motel/cruise package agreements with more than two dozen hotels in the Chicago area, including hotels in downtown Chicago and at O'Hare International Airport. If you want to stay close to the casino, try the Holiday Inn–Joliet, which offers a room for two, cruise tickets and transportation to the casino for $89 (815-729-2000). Some other lodging: Fairfield Inn–Joliet, $52 (815-436-6577); Red Roof Inn, $47 (815-741-2304). To get a detailed accommodations directory for Chicagoland, call 800-223-0121.

Other Reasons to Be Here: See the listing for the Empress Casino, Joliet.

Hollywood Casino

Aurora, Illinois
800-888-7777
708-801-7000

Getting There: In downtown Aurora, look for the New York Street Bridge. The Hollywood pavilion is on an island in the center of the Fox River. From Chicago, take the Burlington-Northern's Metro to the end of the line, then hitch a ride on the free shuttle bus to the casino.

First Impression: Toy boats, but dazzling dock.

Overview: To reverse the old adage, Aurora is a nice place to live, but you wouldn't want to visit there. Close enough to Chicago (about 40 miles) to be a bedroom community, Aurora has some charming residential areas and outlying parks, but its core city is fighting a losing battle with urban decay. The Hollywood Casino, which opened in 1993, is part of a restoration effort that is taking place in a downtown area around the Paramount Theatre, a great movie palace that was restored to its former splendor more than a decade ago. The casino took its theme from the theater, which is about a block away on the river walk.

The Hollywood's pavilion may be the most lavish for a casino in Illinois. The four-story brick structure sits on an island in the center of the muddy Fox River. Inside, it looks something like a nightclub set for a Fred Astaire/Ginger Rogers movie. It's very Art Deco, with swirling staircases, a tall, domed atrium and lots of hot pastel colors and wonderful old-style murals depicting languid movie vamps. Old movie posters are everywhere, along with a little showcase area that displays mementos like Donald O'Connor's shoes from *Singin' in the Rain* and a black lace bustier that was worn by Jean Harlow.

The pavilion houses three fine-dining restaurants, plus an elaborate buffet eating area, a deli, and three bars—including a very upscale lounge called Club Harlow. Parking at a nearby ramp is free, but you have to remember to get your parking ticket validated at the casino's ticket counter.

The Boats: The Hollywood Casino operates two identical boats, The *City of Lights I* and *City of Lights II*, from individual docking facilities on each side of the pavilion. Passengers can enter from three levels. The boats look like interchangeable set pieces for a film version of *Huckleberry Finn*. Technically, they are riverboats, though they travel about as fast as a barge powered by a trolling motor. A spillway just below the pavilion prevents the boats from cruising downriver, and overhead power lines farther upstream would be clipped by the boats' phony smokestacks if they ventured too far in that direction. So they merely push off from the pavilion and hover about 50 yards in midstream. The boats are small (length 145 feet, beam 45 feet) but four decks provide about 10,000 square feet of gaming areas.

The Casinos: You can enter the boats from three levels, each representing a higher investment. The main level has quarter slots and $5 minimum table games. As you ascend, so do the minimums. Each deck is essentially one room of games, with drinks served by "cast members" who are dressed like theater ushers. There's an outside deck on each level, in case you need air. The top deck, with its central bar, is a good place to take a breather without going outside. These are small boats, but especially comfortable in moderate weather.

Cruises: Every 90 minutes, starting at 8:30 A.M.; two hours of cruising, one hour dockside. Admission: Free (at 8:30 A.M.) to $15 for weekend evenings.

In Play: 300 slot and video games (video poker), quarter to $100 machines. 22 blackjack tables ($5–unlimited), using eight-deck shoes (two splits allowed for three hands, with double downs permitted after splitting, except aces). Four craps tables ($5–unlimited), using standard Las Vegas layout. Four roulette tables ($5–unlimited). One mini-baccarat table ($5–unlimited, 5 percent commission).

Specials: Many promotional specials throughout the year, including cash drawings and other prizes. Two-tier slot club offers merchandise, free dinners and other perks. VIP lounge for prime players.

Amenities: The Hollywood Epic Buffet ($3.99 breakfast, $7.77 lunch, $9.99 dinner) features prime rib and shrimp in the evening and provides seating next to huge floor-to-ceiling windows on the river. Rudolfo's Restaurant is a mid-priced Italian eatery. Fairbanks, an upscale steak house, features a 48-ounce Porterhouse steak. Café Harlow, the pavilion's top-line restaurant, specializes in "Cuisine Americain." The pavilion also has two bars: the Director's Lounge, which features tables under a dome, and Harlow's, where the river can be viewed through large arched windows. The casino also books big-name entertainers at the Paramount Arts Center. Past headliners have included Frank Sinatra, Ann-Margret and Tom Jones.

The best deal is the 8:30 A.M. cruise, which is free and also includes a free buffet breakfast before boarding.

Overnight: The Best Western/Fox Valley Inn ($44 single) offers a fitness center, outdoor swimming pool and a restaurant/lounge with nightly entertainment (708-851-2000). Casino patrons with deeper pockets often stay at the more plush Hyatt in nearby Lisle, $99–$124, (800-233-1234).

Other Reasons to Be Here: The Hollywood Casino, like the casinos in Elgin and Joliet, is a Chicagoland attraction. Those who stay near Aurora should take time to admire some of the downtown architecture, including the Old Second National Bank. If you're traveling with children, spend some time at SciTech, a hands-on science center at 18 West Benton St., or go to Blackberry Farm Village (708-892-1550), which features a historical farm, petting zoo and train rides. The Aurora Historical Museum at Cedar and Oak streets (708-897-9029) is housed in a Victorian home, featuring historic furnishings and room settings; admission is free.

Par•A•Dice Riverboat Casino

East Peoria, Illinois
800-727-2342

Getting There: From Interstate 74, take Exit 94B to Highway 116, then follow the signs to the casino.

First Impression: Getting bigger, and needs it.

Overview: "Will it play in Peoria?" is an old show-biz quip about solid, if somewhat dull, Midwestern tastes. Actually, Peoria is the third largest city in Illinois, with a population of nearly 250,000, and a history that goes back to French traders. Like the other sites for Illinois casino boats, Peoria also is an aging industrial community, begging for economic revitalization. The casino opened in 1991 and moved a year later to its present pavilion berth on the east side of the Illinois River. It's part of a hospitality-industry boom that generated more than $100 million in spending in 1992. The Par•a•Dice is one of the most heavily promoted casinos in the Midwest, but it's also part of a big local tourism industry that includes several highly regarded museums and wildlife parks.

The Boat: In 1994, the Par•a•Dice acquired a new, $20 million casino boat from the Atlantic Marine shipyard in Florida. The sleek, four-deck cruise-type boat is 240 feet long, with a beam of 66 feet and a height of nearly 67 feet. It has 33,000 square feet of casino space and can carry 1,600 passengers. It docks at the casino's pavilion, which has two restaurants—the Broadway Buffet and Boulevard Grill—and the Flappers Lounge. The only downside to the facility is its lack of an adequate indoor waiting area; during summer, however, the outdoor picnic lounge is enchanting and sunny.

The Casino: The new boat has three decks for gaming, including a second-deck atrium with a balcony above. Each deck has a bar and the third deck has a small deli. The top-side "hurricane deck" has lounge tables for warm-weather seating. The slot machines range from 21 nickel machines to a single $100 machine. Most take quarters (475 of them) or dollars (277). The high denomination machines are on the first deck; the nickel slots are on the third deck's balcony area. The first cruise, at 9 A.M., features low-minimum table games where you can play for $3 a bet. The minimum is $5 for all other sessions. As with most Illinois boats, high-rollers can ask for unlimited betting.

Cruises: 6 daily. Each cruise is two hours, for a three-hour gaming session. Admission: $4 to $9.

In Play: 791 slot and video games (video poker, keno), nickel to one $100 machine. 32 blackjack tables ($5–$2,000), using six-deck shoes. Five craps tables ($5–$2,000), offering double odds and using standard Las Vegas layouts. Three roulette tables ($5–$2,000). One mini-baccarat table ($5–$2,000).

Specials: Blackjack tournaments. From January through April, the casino sells a Preferred Pass for $9.95 that provides free admission to the boat, plus discounts at the two restaurants. It's a bargain if you take more than one cruise.

Amenities: The casino's brick-and-glass pavilion has two restaurants and an entertainment lounge. The Par•a•Dice Club card rewards gambling with merchandise; joining the club opens the way to an avalanche of promotional mail. The casino also books major entertainers into the Peoria Civic Center; tickets are sold at the casino (800-847-7117). The Par•a•Dice offers a bewildering array of special discounts and packages, including a senior discount on Mondays, free cruises for women on Tuesdays and free cruises for men on Thursdays. Groups receive coupon fun books and other inducements.

Overnight: The closest hotel is a Hampton Inn located on the opposite side of the casino's parking lot. The hotel has 151 rooms, complimentary breakfasts, and it offers casino packages that include a room for two and two cruise tickets, $66–$76 (309-694-0711). The Red Roof Inn Peoria, 4031 N. War Memorial Drive, is recommended by Frommer's, $42 (800-843-7663). Peoria has scores of motels and hotels; call the Peoria Convention and Visitors Bureau (309-676-0303) for details.

Other Reasons to Be Here: Peoria's 2,000-acre Wildlife Prairie Park (309-676-0998) is an Illinois heritage park recognized by the National Park Service. The Lakeview Museum, 1125 Lake Ave., has set up the largest model of the solar system in the world, with the sun at the museum and Pluto in Kewanee, about 40 miles away (309-686-7000). The Wheels O' Time Museum, 11923 N. Knoxville St., is an excellent stop for fans of autos, clocks, models and trains (309-243-9020). And, lastly, the Illinois Historical Water Museum, 123 S.W. Washington (309-671-3744), is housed in a building festooned with turrets and gargoyles. If you're interested in the history of water, this is the place to go—though you should also know that the museum has been featured in the offbeat book, *Roadside America's Boring Tour.*

Players Riverboat Casino

Metropolis, Illinois
800-929-5970
618-524-2628

Getting There: From Interstate 24 to Metropolis, take Exit 37 and follow the signs to the casino.

First Impression: A boat for the people—including those with nickels.

Overview: Metropolis, located just across the river from Paducah, Ky., at the bottom of Illinois, is the self-proclaimed home of Superman. Once saddled with failed businesses and an unemployment rate of 17 percent, the town of 7,000 is now home to one of Illinois' most successful riverboat casinos. In 1993, when the community decided to erect a new, 15-foot Superman statue in Superman Square, somebody suggested that the Man of Steel ought to look like Merv Griffin, a partner in Players Riverboat Casino. The casino, which came to Metropolis early in 1993, has sparked a tremendous building boom that includes a dozen trendy restaurants and bars, dozens of antique and curio shops, the Merv Griffin Theater and a casino-owned, land-based hotel.

The Boat: The casino is a 1,400-passenger, 210-foot replica of a nineteenth-century sidewheeler, decorated to look like an amusement-park version of the boats that steamed down the Ohio River when Mark Twain was a boy. The three-deck craft docks at Merv Griffin Landing, a permanently moored complex that also houses the Celebrity Buffet, where the walls are decorated with Hollywood star photos that are said to come from Griffin's personal collection. Merv's Bar & Grill, also part of the on-shore complex, has a 40-foot solid mahogany bar and windows that face the Ohio River. The site also has a 1,000-car parking lot.

The Casino: Theoretically, the sky's the limit, but the reality is that Players is a place for purse-pinchers—at least during the day. Nickel slot machines are big here. The average patron typically spends less than $50 per cruise, served by casino employees who are handsomely turned out in 1870s period costumes. On weekend nights, the atmosphere shifts as younger gamblers—many of them more reckless—arrive on the scene. Unlike other Illinois boats, Players has a distinctly Southern clientele, many from Missouri and Kentucky. A large percentage of the patrons come from Tennessee, where Nashville and Clarksville are major markets.

Cruises: Five per weekday, six on weekends. Each cruise is two hours, for a three-hour gaming session. Admission: $2–$12.

In Play: 630 slot and video games (video poker, keno), nickel to $25 machines. 30 blackjack tables ($2–$500), using three-deck shoes. Five craps tables ($2–$500), two roulette tables ($2–$500). One Big Six Wheel.

Specials: Monthly slot tournaments. Regular blackjack tournaments. Higher bet limits can be negotiated. Player ratings, including a Player Preferred card that rewards slot play with merchandise.

Amenities: Liquor served. Dining and bar facilities at Merv Griffin's Landing. Jazz and Dixieland bands perform during warm months. Headliner entertainers at the Merv Griffin Theater.

Overnight: A casino-owned hotel was expected to open by mid-summer 1994. Call the casino for details. Rates vary widely at Metropolis inns according to the season. Best Inns of America, 2055 Fifth St., (800-237-8466) has 63 rooms, an outdoor swimming pool and complimentary breakfast. The Days Inn Motel, Routes 45 and 3 (618-524-9341), also offers outdoor swimming. Other lodging: the American Inn, 1502 W. 10th St. (618-524-7431); the Metropolis Inn Motel, Highway 45 and 24 (618-524-3723).

Other Reasons to Be Here: Metropolis is the gateway to Western Kentucky and Nashville. Kentucky Lake, a major recreation area, is less than an hour away. It's a three-hour trip from Metropolis to Mammoth Cave National Park in Kentucky, but the drive is worth it; tours of the world's largest cave are scheduled all day. Legendary Nashville is about 200 miles away.

Silver Eagle Casino Cruise

East Dubuque, Illinois
800-745-8371

Getting There: Just off Highway 20, about two miles east of the Mississippi River bridge.

First Impression: Sleek, compact and comfortable.

Overview: Dubuque is a great old river town, notable for its Victorian homes, its many small colleges and for attractions that range from grand opera to downhill skiing. Dubuque also is notable because few pass through it on the way to somewhere else; there are no interstate highways slicing through the city. Less than an hour's drive east is Galena, Ill., home of President U.S. Grant, and one of the best-preserved nineteenth-century towns in America.

The greater Dubuque area now has two riverboat casinos—the Illinois-based *Silver Eagle* in the formerly rough-and-tumble suburb of East Dubuque, and the *Dubuque Diamond Jo*, which opened on the Iowa side of the river in 1994. If that isn't enough, you can also visit the Dubuque Greyhound Park (800-373-3647), which is open from April through October.

The Boat: The *Silver Eagle* is berthed in a marina that can be reached from a frontage road off Highway 20. The pavilion is a neatly maintained, faux-limestone building with a low-slung, blue-metal roof. Inside, it's a spacious place, with a bar lounge called Talons, a buffet restaurant called Wings, plus a small snack bar and gift shop. The boat is a cruise-styled vessel that looks fairly small; actually, it's a 205-footer, with three decks and a sundeck. Aboard, it's a pleasant surprise, designed for space. The second deck is an atrium mezzanine, where there's a dandy place to stand and spy on the craps table one deck below. Windows ring each deck and the stern of the boat has terrific lounges on two levels, serving a formal light buffet.

The Casino: There seems to be something unhurried about the Silver Eagle. Perhaps it has to do with the amount of space set aside for lounging. The frantic, loud activity of some boats isn't apparent here. Among the electronic games, there appears to be an emphasis on video poker; in fact, nearly a third of all the slots are video poker machines. Video keno is another emphasized game. The third level of the boat has a walkabout deck, and it's here that you can find nickel slot and video poker machines.

Cruises: Six cruises daily, starting at 8:30 A.M. Each cruise is two hours of cruising, for a gaming session of three hours.

In Play: 370 slot and video games (video poker, keno), nickel to $5 machines. 20 blackjack tables ($3–unlimited, dealer hits on soft 17s). Three craps tables ($5–unlimited) using a standard Las Vegas layout. Two roulette tables ($5–unlimited).

Specials: Regular blackjack tournaments. Rated players. Slot club.

Amenities: Two lounges aboard the boat serving light snacks, plus a third-level bar. Restaurant and deli in pavilion. Entertainment offered monthly on boat and in the pavilion.

Overnight: Eagle Ridge Inn and Resort in Galena has a management relationship with the casino. A two-night, three-meal (including dinner) package for two includes cruise tickets and costs $220–$235 per person (800-892-2269). Otherwise, there are literally hundreds of inns, motels, resorts and B&Bs in the Dubuque/Galena area. Among the inns are the Oakcrest Guest Homes, which feature great rooms with fireplaces that cost about $70 per person (319-582-4207). The Hancock House, $75–$150, is a nine-room inn in an old Victorian house in Dubuque (319-557-8989). For additional information, call the Dubuque Convention and Visitors Bureau (800-798-8844).

Other Reasons to Be Here: Crystal Lake Cave, located about five miles south of Dubuque, is considered one of the great show caves in America (319-556-6451). In Dubuque the 1889 Grand Opera House, which once billed performances by George M. Cohan, Lillian Russell, Ethel Barrymore and Sarah Bernhardt, still operates today (319-588-4356). Ski at Chestnut Mountain Resort (800-798-0098) or Sundown Mountain (319-556-6676). The Mathias Ham House Historic Site (319-583-2812), reflects the splendor of antebellum Dubuque. And just for fun, ride the Fenelon Place Elevator, the world's shortest, steepest, scenic railway, from Fourth Street to Fenelon Place (319-582-6496).

CHAPTER 3

IOWA

The Name of the Game: The gambling industry in Iowa stuck its collective head into a kitchen blender in 1994 and flipped the switch. At the time this book is being written, no one is quite sure about the results. But it's possible that gambling in Iowa is about to enter a period of booming growth.

In 1991, Iowa became the first state to allow riverboat casinos. Since then, three Indian casinos also have opened in the state. And in 1994, the legislature allowed Iowa's dog tracks and the Prairie Meadows horse track in Altoona to install slot machines. Under Iowa law, the Indian casinos and riverboats are "full service" operations. They have slot and video machines, poker rooms, and all the traditional table games: blackjack, roulette, craps and red dog, a high-low card game. Two of the three Indian casinos have keno parlors and the Mesquaki Casino in east-central Iowa runs a horse racing book. Baccarat is legal, but the game isn't popular and it's unlikely that you'll see it played.

Until 1994, Iowa had some peculiar regulations pertaining to gambling. Bets were limited to $5, and a loss limit of $200 in three hours required all casinos to have check-in counters and issue money receipts to their customers.

In addition to the bet and loss restrictions, riverboats had to limit gambling to 30 percent of deck space. Gamblers could board the boat only at specified times and if the boat wasn't cruising, anybody who got off during the gambling session couldn't get back on. The minimum age to gamble was 18.

The restrictions—especially bet and loss limits—made it difficult for Iowa boats to compete with their no-limit counterparts in Illinois. So in 1994, the legislature radically changed the rules for riverboats in a way that will make Iowa more attractive to riverboat gamblers. In terms of bets,

Iowa is now a no-limit state. The minimum age to gamble has been raised to 21. The size of gaming areas on boats is not restricted by law, but only by maritime safety standards.

But more significantly, perhaps, the boats are free from rules on boarding and cruising. When the casino boat is docked, gamblers can come and go as they please. How important was this change about boarding? In the first week after the change in boarding rules, the number of customers boarding the casino boat in Clinton increased by 3,000. Iowa still requires riverboats to cruise during warm weather, but it's likely that most of the boats will cruise as little as once a day and operate as walk-on casinos the rest of the time.

The changes have produced a surge of enthusiasm for riverboat casinos. At the time of this writing, new riverboats have been proposed in Fort Madison in southeastern Iowa, Council Bluffs in western Iowa and Marquette, a little town in northeastern Iowa that's across the river from Prairie du Chien, Wis. The new *Dubuque Diamond Jo* is scheduled to open in the summer of 1994, and larger boats were scheduled to replace the riverboats in Clinton and Sioux City.

Meanwhile, the opening of race tracks to slot machines is expected to produce big crowds at the tracks. By the time you read this, Iowa's Prairie Meadows horse track in Altoona will probably have a slot casino with as many as 1,000 machines. Slot parlors also will be part of the dog tracks at Dubuque and Council Bluffs.

Iowa's big change in gambling rules also means that you'll see subtle or significant changes in every casino. The elimination of bet limits should prompt some casinos to emphasize games that have more betting churn—such as craps and roulette—and to install more blackjack tables. The slot areas probably won't change much (why throw out all those money-making machines?), but new machines are likely to have higher denominations.

Lamentably, it's likely that quarter craps and quarter roulette will disappear. In order to play those games, you'll probably have to invest more money. At many casinos, however, it's possible that you'll see little change. Gambling in Iowa continues to be typified by low-investment players—ordinary folks on limited budgets who are out for a few hours of fun.

The Rules of the Game: Casino gambling in Iowa is mainly a border activity. Casinos operate along the Mississippi River border with Wisconsin and Illinois and along the Missouri River border with Nebraska.

Two of the three Indian casinos—WinnaVegas and CasinOmaha—are operated by Nebraska tribes. Both are just south of Sioux City on the Nebraska border. The only interior casino is the Mesquaki Bingo and Casino in north-central Iowa, about 50 miles from Des Moines. In 1993, it was one of the biggest tourist destinations in the state—beating out Herbert

Hoover's birthplace in West Branch, the clock museum in Spillville and even the commercial bullhead fishery in Spirit Lake.

None of these places has the glitz that you find in larger casinos in Illinois, Minnesota or Wisconsin. The fanciest boat, the *President* in Davenport, is more like a handsome floating antique than an upscale den of iniquity.

On the other hand, Iowa casinos don't have the rough edges that you see in northern Wisconsin, northern Minnesota or North Dakota. Like their boats and Iowans in general, these are even-keel places.

CasinOmaha

Onawa, Iowa
800-858-8238
712-423-3700

Getting There: From Interstate 29 take the exit for Onawa, then go west, following the signs that lead you on a winding, five-mile route to the casino.

First Impression: The oasis syndrome.

Overview: Onawa is almost midway between Omaha and Sioux City. The neat little community's biggest attraction is Lewis and Clark State Park, with its replica of a keelboat used by explorers.

The Casino: Once you find it, you may be disappointed by the outward appearance of CasinOmaha, which is a strange, wedge-shaped building with a purple and yellow canopy, sitting in the middle of cornfields. Inside, however, it's much bigger than you expected. It's also very dark, illuminated by palm leaf-shaped neon lights. Everything is in one big room, divided by ramps and chin-high partitions that are topped with etched glass. It's an example of a small room benefiting from upscale treatment.

Compared to WinnaVegas, just 20 minutes away, this is a high-buck place. There are no nickel slots, and there are plenty of 50-cent machines. The restaurant buffet and bar are sequestered from the gaming area. There's also a walk-up snack bar. It's a very business-like place, tightly organized, and it probably draws a lot of patrons from Omaha. Bus tours and other group promotions appear to be a bread-and-butter constituency.

Hours: 24 daily.

In Play: Slots and video games, craps, roulette, blackjack, table poker, Big Six Wheel.

Specials: Many discount group programs. The Onawa Chamber of Commerce provides free coupon books for the casino.

Amenities: Buffet restaurant and snack bar, full liquor bar.

Overnight: The Riverboat Inn in Sioux City, $49–$53, offers casino specials (800-238-6146). Two bed-and-breakfast inns in Missouri Valley, about 35 miles south, are recommended: Apple Orchard Inn, $65 (712-642-2418), which is near the DeSoto Bend Wildlife Refuge; and the Hilltop Bed & Breakfast, $55–$65 (712-642-3695), which also is part of an apple orchard.

Other Reasons to Be Here: The keelboat replica at Lewis and Clark State Park is open in warm months (712-423-2829). The Kiwanis Museum Complex in Onawa is a restored Chicago & North Western Railway depot with more than 700 items of railroad memorabilia. Nearby is a country school, restored to look as it did in the 1800s, plus a country church that was built by Swedish immigrants.

Catfish Bend Casinos

Fort Madison, Iowa
Burlington, Iowa
800-372-2946
319-372-2946
(Opening Fall 1994)

Getting There: Burlington is 20 miles north of Fort Madison.

Overview: The *Mississippi Belle II*, which docked for many years in Clinton, was scheduled to move downriver to Fort Madison in the fall of 1994 and begin operation under the new name of Catfish Bend Casinos. The boat will operate from docks in Fort Madison during the summer months and return to Burlington for the winter. Call ahead for more information.

The Boat: Because of safety restrictions, it's not likely that the boat will carry more gaming areas than she had while cruising from Clinton. She is a small, first-generation craft, built in 1986 as an excursion boat and converted in 1991. When aboard, you know you're on a boat.

In Play: Approximately 260 slot machines, nine blackjack tables, one craps table, one roulette table. While cruising from Clinton, the boat had a large dining and dancing area on the first deck, a full boiler deck casino and an active poker room in the small enclosed area of the third deck.

Amenities: On-board dining is expected to continue.

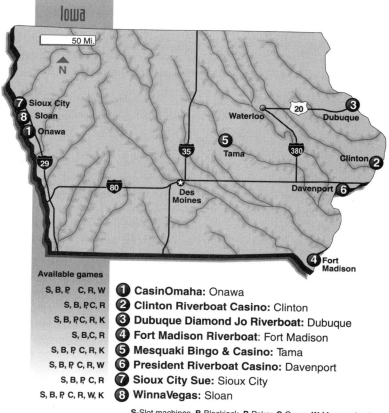

Iowa

50 Mi.

N

7 Sioux City
8 Sloan
1 Onawa

Waterloo

20

Dubuque **3**

5
Tama

35

380

Clinton **2**

29

80

Des
Moines

Davenport **6**

4 Fort
Madison

Available games

S, B, P, C, R, W	**1** **CasinOmaha:** Onawa
S, B, P,C, R	**2** **Clinton Riverboat Casino:** Clinton
S, B, P,C, R, K	**3** **Dubuque Diamond Jo Riverboat:** Dubuque
S, B,C, R	**4** **Fort Madison Riverboat:** Fort Madison
S, B, P, C, R, K	**5** **Mesquaki Bingo & Casino:** Tama
S, B, P, C, R, W	**6** **President Riverboat Casino:** Davenport
S, B, P, C, R	**7** **Sioux City Sue:** Sioux City
S, B, P, C, R, W, K	**8** **WinnaVegas:** Sloan

S-Slot machines, **B**-Blackjack, **P**-Poker, **C**-Craps, **W**-Money wheel,
R-Roulett, **M**-Mini Baccarat

Overnight: The Best Western Iowan Motor Lodge in Fort Madison is a full-service facility, $45–$75 (800-528-1234 or 319-372-7510). Also consider the Super 8 Motel, $35–$65 (319-372-8500).

Other Reasons to Be Here: The Old Fort Madison Historical Site recreates nineteenth-century life at the old fort. Situated on the Mississippi, the fort is part of Riverview Park, which has a marina, boat rentals and other recreational activities, plus the Santa Fe steam locomotive and Old Chimney Monument (319-372-6318). The North Lee County Historical Center (319-372-7661) is a registered National Historic site.

Clinton Riverboat Casino

Clinton, Iowa
800-457-9975
319-243-9000

Getting There: Take Highway 30 or Highway 67 to Clinton. The boat docks at Showboat Landing, two blocks north of Highway 30 on the river.

First Impression: At the old ball game.

Overview: Clinton is a comfortable-sized river town with a modestly developed recreation area along the Mississippi. The new casino boat, scheduled to arrive in September 1994, will dock next to the Clinton Area Showboat Theater, a permanently moored barge that houses the local civic and summer stock theaters. The showboat serves as the casino's ticketing office. Directly across from Showboat Landing is the ballpark for the Clinton Lumber Kings, a Class A farm club of the San Francisco Giants.

The Boat: The new boat has a length of 228 feet and a beam of 64 feet. A replica of a nineteenth-century riverboat, it is roughly twice the size of Clinton's old boat, *Mississippi Belle II*, which was scheduled to move downriver to the Fort Madison area. The owners expect the new Clinton Riverboat Casino to cruise as little as once a day during the season and to operate as a free-access casino the rest of the time.

In Play: Two-deck gaming area, carrying 518 slot and video games, 20 blackjack tables, four poker tables, two craps tables, two roulette tables. Clinton is a "grind town," and operators of the new boat do not expect it to operate as a high-stakes casino.

Amenities: The third deck will house a 300-seat restaurant. Liquor served.

Overnight: The Best Western Frontier Motor Inn, with 117 units, is one of Clinton's largest hotels, $57 (800-728-7112). Think about driving south along scenic (though narrow) Highway 67 toward the Quad Cities. At LeClaire, you'll find two nice bed-and-breakfast inns: The Country Inn Bed & Breakfast, which has a swimming pool and elaborate gardens, $50–$75 (319-289-4793); and Mississippi Sunrise Bed & Breakfast, which has an acre of gardens and an enclosed porch and deck, under $50 (319-332-9203).

Other Reasons to Be Here: The Bickelhaupt Arboretum features a collection of roses, wildflowers, prairie grasses and rare trees and is open all year from dawn to dusk (319-242-4771). Check out the theater offerings at the Clinton Area Showboat Theatre (319-242-6760) or see if the Clinton Lumber Kings are playing a home game (319-242-0727). For the kids, the Soaring Eagles Nature Center features live animals, birds of prey, animal petting and feeding areas, plus walking trails (319-242-9088). Also check out the Clinton Art Association Gallery and Pottery School (319-243-3300) and the Clinton County Historical Society Museum (319-242-1201).

Dubuque Diamond Jo

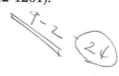

Dubuque, Iowa
800-582-5956
319-583-7005

The Boat: When it opens, the Dubuque Diamond Jo will compete directly with the Silver Eagle Casino in East Dubuque, Ill. Construction delays postponed the opening of the casino, which once had been promised for 1993. The advantages created by Iowa's new gaming regulations may benefit this casino, whenever it arrives.

Overnight: See listings for the Silver Eagle Casino, East Dubuque, Ill.

Mesquaki Bingo and Casino

Tama, Iowa
800-728-4263

Getting There: On Highway 30, about five miles west of Tama and Toledo in east-central Iowa.

First Impression: Too small, but has it all.

Overview: The Mesquaki Bingo and Casino was one of the biggest tourist destinations in Iowa in 1993, principally because it has a lock on the gambling market in central Iowa. Unfortunately, the building has a maximum occupancy limit of 1,500, but gets nearly 4,500 visitors on weekdays and more than 7,000 patrons on weekends. On weekends, it's not unusual to see up to 150 people standing outside, waiting to get in. Not surprisingly, the Mesquaki tribe is committed to a major expansion, including a 145,000-square-foot addition with a 300-seat buffet. Nearest city: Des Moines, about 50 miles east and south.

The Casino: This casino has a little of everything, including a horse-racing book, a large poker room, a small sit-down area for paper keno, and a 450-seat bingo hall. As a result, everything is terribly crowded. Some of the slot areas are stand-only aisles; in others you can lean backward and brace yourself against the back of the person sitting behind you. There's only enough room for a single down-sized craps table and one roulette operation, plus a dozen blackjack tables. The poker room is sequestered from the throng, but reservations are advised.

Hours: 24 daily.

In Play: 575 slot and video games (video poker, keno). Blackjack, craps, roulette, poker (Texas Hold 'Em, seven-card stud, Omaha). Horse racing book. Keno parlor.

Amenities: The food areas are confined to two fast-food snack bars, though the daily breakfast is recommended. No liquor. Shuttle services to some motels in Tama and Toledo.

Overnight: The casino provides shuttle services to several area motels, including the Super 8 in Tama, $44, (515-484-5888). For a list of other motels within shuttle distance, call the casino.

Other Reasons to Be Here: The Amana Colonies are about 75 miles away, offering dozens of lodges, shops and restaurants, plus a glimpse of one of America's most successful communal societies. Don't leave the Tama area without visiting the Lincoln Highway Bridge on old Route 30; constructed in 1915, it's on the National Historic Register. Also visit the Tama County Historical Museum in Toledo (515-484-6767) to see an interesting collection of Indian and pioneer artifacts.

The President Riverboat Casino

Davenport, Iowa
800-262-8711
319-322-2578

Getting There: From Iowa, exit Interstate 80 on Highway 61 and drive to the Mississippi River. From Illinois, take Interstate 280 to the Centennial Freeway (Highway 92), cross the Centennial Bridge (50-cent toll) and turn right.

First Impression: A real riverboat.

Overview: Davenport is part of the Quad Cities area that also includes Bettendorf in Iowa and Rock Island and Moline in Illinois. Riverboat gambling has been here since it became legal in 1991, and it was speculated shortly after Iowa liberalized its gaming rules in 1994 that a second Iowa boat would dock in nearby Bettendorf by 1995. Rock Island has the smaller, highly upscale *Casino Rock Island*, directly across the river from the *President*.

The Boat: The *President* is a huge boat, as long as a football field and 87 feet at the beam. She also has the distinction of being a National Historic Landmark, the last remaining packet boat on the Upper Mississippi. The hull was laid in Cincinnati in 1924, when she was a sidewheel passenger steamboat. Over the years, she moved to St. Louis and New Orleans. After a $10 million renovation in 1989, she became the first casino riverboat to open under Iowa's 1991 riverboat gaming system.

The pavilion for the *President* was created by welding together two barges to create a floating platform big enough to hold a modest-sized cafeteria snack bar and a huge bar lounge called the Mark Twain.

The *President* has five decks, including a 200-seat buffet restaurant and large, 10-table poker room on the fourth deck (the owners plan to renovate this deck extensively). Part of the engine deck is reserved for kids; clowns and other entertainers put on shows here on weekends, and the area has a few video games and lots of deck space for running. Overall, the boat can carry up to 3,000 passengers, but the crowds are usually kept to about 1,800.

The Casino: The main gaming area of the *President* is a second-deck salon with 20-foot ceilings and a third-deck balcony. The surroundings are ornate, from murals to gilt-edged ceiling panels. The games, which include a bewildering variety of blackjack variations, will probably change because of new betting rules. But because of weight restrictions, its unlikely that those changes will significantly alter the number of slot machines.

The *President* is the place to experiment with strange table-game variations. These include "double exposure" blackjack, where the dealer's cards are dealt face-up; multi-action blackjack, where the player wagers up to three bets against three different dealer hands; Super 7, where jackpots are paid if the player makes a side bet on getting multiple 7s; and over/under 13, where you can make side bets on getting less than 13 or more than 13 on your first two cards.

In Play: About 700 slot and video games, blackjack, red dog, craps, roulette, and Big Six Wheel. Poker room.

Specials: The Captain's Club returns one coin for every $2 played in a slot machine, and one coin for every $3 played in a poker machine. In the past, the *President* offered all kinds of gambling packages and other specials.

Amenities: Restaurant, bars, area for children. A fee is charged for parking.

Overnight: Full-service hotels with pools and restaurants include the Best Western Riverview Inn (800-528-1234 or 319-324-1921) and the Best Western SteepleGate Inn (319-386-6900); the Blackhawk Hotel (319-323-2711) and the Days Inn (319-355-1190). All charge between $35 and $75. The Bishop's House Inn in Davenport is a sumptuous Italianate mansion filled with antiques and stained glass, but also outfitted with whirlpool tubs, $75 and up (319-324-2454).

Other Reasons to Be Here: See the listing for *Casino Rock Island*, Ill.

Sioux City Sue

Sioux City, Iowa
800-424-0080

Getting There: From Interstate 29 in Sioux City, take the Hamilton Street exit and follow the frontage road along the Missouri River to the casino. The boat is just south of the main expressway bridge to Nebraska.

First Impression: Needs help.

Overview: Sioux City has some of the nicest elements of western prairie and river culture. Parts of the city are lovely and gracious, though many visitors who pass through the city on the interstate highway see little more than the stockyards and industrial areas.

Sioux City Sue has struggled since opening in the river area near a new pavilion and museum boat. For one thing, the casino boat is the smallest in the state and was scheduled to be replaced by a larger boat in 1994. These plans are now on hold.

Sioux City Sue also has the misfortune of being too close to two large Indian casinos—WinnaVegas, just 25 miles south of Sioux City; and Casin-Omaha, just 15 miles farther south. To make matters worse, a strip of some 100, small-time gambling joints (10 video lottery machines each) operates just northwest of Sioux City, on the South Dakota side of the river.

The Boat: *Sioux City Sue* is a short, narrow, three-deck riverboat, with narrow little gambling areas and a top-side poker room that is very popular with the locals.

In Play: Slots and video games, blackjack, craps, roulette, poker.

Overnight: Marina Inn in South Sioux City, Neb., is admired for its lovely restaurant, which has fabulous views of the river, $60–$75 (402-494-4000 or 800-798-7980). Other lodging: The Holiday Inn, $49–$63 double (712-277-3211 or 800-274-3211); the Riverboat Inn has double queen-bed rooms and a restaurant, $49–$53 (800-238-6146 or 712-277-9400).

Other Reasons to Be Here: The Sergeant Floyd Riverboat Museum, located near the casino boat, is a dry-docked diesel inspection boat that plied the Missouri River for 50 years as the flagship of the U.S. Army Corps of Engineers; it's now filled with artifacts of river history, along with a welcome center and gift shop (712-279-4840). The Sioux City Public Museum (712-279-6174) is housed in the 1893 Pierce Mansion, a marvelous castle structure that features displays on natural history, anthropology and military history. Bacon Creek Park (712-279-6126) is a great summer destination, with paddleboats and 34 acres of walking paths. K.D. Station (712-277-8787) combines a museum of meat-packing history (no kidding!) with restaurants, bowling and miniature golf.

WinnaVegas

Sloan, Iowa
712-428-9466

Getting There: Take Interstate 29 about 20 miles south of Sioux City and exit at Sloan. Go west about three miles until the road ends at the casino.

First Impression: A full-service "grind joint."

Overview: Sloan is a pleasant little farm town, but you'll never see it unless you make a wrong turn after exiting I-29 and go east instead of west. This is major corn-belt country, with roads as straight as a taut string. Winna-Vegas appears suddenly—an enormous beige-colored building with the usual oversized parking lot. A separate entrance allows parents with kids to reach the buffet restaurant. For all its size, WinnaVegas still has a small-town attitude. That makes sense: This is a small town.

The Casino: This is Iowa's biggest casino, built in 1993. It seeks low-budget players by offering lots of nickel slot machines, a low-price-big-selection buffet and a big-time keno parlor. The hall itself is a large rectangular space with a few small alcoves. The poker room is crowded, smoky and not for the amateur. But perhaps the finest feature is a splendid, double-sided roulette table, a real showpiece with the wheel in the center.

The keno parlor offers a bewildering selection of number options, from the standard 1–15 grouping, to 16- and 20-number "never lose" games, to a 190-way, eight-spot game that requires a minimum wager of $19. Most people play the $1 combinations, since they still qualify for a $100,000 jackpot.

Roulette and craps were low-end games here until the change in Iowa's betting and loss limits. It's likely that the number of tables will increase, along with the wager minimums, though the casino will continue to market itself as a place for low-investment gamblers.

Hours: 24 daily.

In Play: More than 700 slot and video games (video poker, keno). Craps, roulette, blackjack, red dog, table poker, Big Six Wheel, keno.

Amenities: Buffet restaurant serves all meals, plus a Sunday brunch. 24-hour snack bar. Alcohol served from a central bar, though there's not a big emphasis on drinking in the gaming area.

Overnight: Try Elaine's Lighthouse Marina Inn in Whiting, part of a fishing and camping resort along the Missouri River, $60 (712-458-2066). For other lodging, check the overnight suggestions under the listing for *Sioux City Sue*.

C H A P T E R 4

MINNESOTA

The Rules of the Game: When a Minneapolis cabaret theater took on the subject of casinos "Minnesota-style," the satirists dreamed up a skit in which James Bond broke the bank at Monte Carlo, but couldn't handle the action at a big, bright, squeaky-clean Minnesota gambling joint.

First, Agent 007 discovered that he couldn't get a martini—let alone one that was shaken, not stirred. And when he started making heavy bets, the dealer, with a look of concern on his face, handed him a brochure for Gamblers Anonymous. Unnerved, Bond allowed himself to be led away to one of Minnesota's 10,000 treatment centers.

Gross exaggeration is a principal weapon in satire. But to be appreciated, it has to contain an element of truth.

With more casinos than Atlantic City, Minnesota is the largest Indian gaming market in the United States. There are 17 Indian-operated casinos in the state, and in 1993 it was estimated that they produced a combined gross revenue of more than $3 billion. The boom has produced some of the biggest casinos in the Midwest. Mystic Lake, the closest casino to Minneapolis/St. Paul, is a sprawling 340,000-square-foot complex. Other casinos larger than 100,000 square feet are taken for granted. With only a few exceptions, it's now possible for anyone in Minnesota to reach a casino within 60 miles of home. All are virtually brand new.

Casino gambling came on the Minnesota scene in the late 1980s and suddenly exploded into a major industry in 1991 with the opening of most of the casinos that exist today. The vast popularity of casino gambling came as a big surprise to those who accepted the general view of Minnesotans as stoic, hard-working Lutherans whose idea of fun is enjoying a second cup of coffee.

But a lot of people knew otherwise. For example, Las Vegas casinos have always viewed Minnesota as a major customer market. Advertising for Las Vegas travel is heavy in the state, and one metropolitan newspaper— the *St. Paul Pioneer Press*—prints a special section about Las Vegas once a month.

But any first-time visitor will instantly notice that casinos in Minnesota have some qualities that are unique. First, there's the issue of alcohol. Many of Minnesota's casinos are dry—including the big Mystic Lake complex. Grand Casino Hinckley, one of the other big casinos, imposes a two-drink limit in its entertainment lounge and donates 50 cents of every drink price to alcohol abuse treatment programs. Some other casinos sell alcoholic beverages, but not in the gaming areas. Only one casino—Jackpot Junction near Redwood Falls—serves complimentary cocktails, but only to players in its private, high-stakes area.

There are no smoke-free casinos in Minnesota, but some have large no-smoking areas. And if you've never visited Minnesota, believe it when a sign says "No Smoking." To blow smoke in a smoke-free zone is to invite a big fine.

Critics of gambling may mutter "hypocrisy," but some casinos are very concerned about gambling addiction. Mystic Lake, for example, made head-lines when it hired a private gambling-treatment agency to train its employ-ees and provide services for some of the casino's problem customers.

At the same time, the casinos employ all the standard techniques to entice premium players. Many use card clubs to track and identify high-volume customers. All try for the bus and limo trade. Most pass out the usual assortment of freebies—though they tend to be quiet about it.

They may not get that drink, but Minnesota gamblers expect their casinos to offer food—and plenty of it. In a dining culture where quality and quan-tity are frequently synonymous, casinos have learned to excel. Many have buffets that are unmatched by any casinos in the Midwest.

And, finally, there's the whole issue of "Minnesota Nice." This is a state where being impolite is worse than just about anything. So Minnesota casinos tend to be friendly. But that cuts both ways: You'd better be friendly, too. And mind your manners.

The Name of the Game: Minnesota currently allows only one table game: blackjack. It's played in the traditional Las Vegas fashion, with the cards dealt face up from shoes that contain between two and eight decks. Except for aces, double downs are permitted after splits at most casinos. Most casinos require dealers to stand on all 17s, though a few allow them to take a hit when the 17 is soft. There are no state-imposed bet limits, though $1,000 is about as high as most casinos are prepared to go, and many put the brakes on at $200 or less.

Technically, Minnesota has no slot machines. Here they are called video gaming devices and they cannot have the traditional mechanical reels.

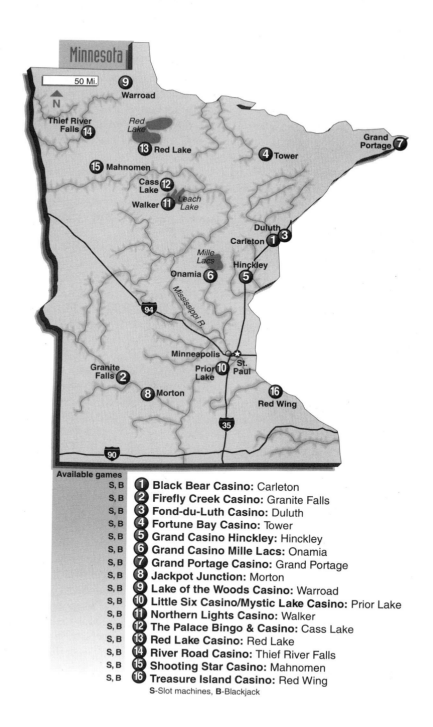

Minnesota

50 Mi.

N

Warroad ⑨

Thief River Falls ⑭

Red Lake

⑬ Red Lake

④ Tower

Grand Portage ⑦

⑮ Mahnomen

Cass Lake ⑫

Walker ⑪ *Leach Lake*

Duluth

Carleton ① ③

Hinckley ⑤

Mille Lacs

Onamia ⑥

94

Mississippi R.

Minneapolis

Prior Lake ⑩

St. Paul

Granite Falls ②

⑧ Morton

⑯

Red Wing

35

90

Available games

S, B	①	**Black Bear Casino:** Carleton
S, B	②	**Firefly Creek Casino:** Granite Falls
S, B	③	**Fond-du-Luth Casino:** Duluth
S, B	④	**Fortune Bay Casino:** Tower
S, B	⑤	**Grand Casino Hinckley:** Hinckley
S, B	⑥	**Grand Casino Mille Lacs:** Onamia
S, B	⑦	**Grand Portage Casino:** Grand Portage
S, B	⑧	**Jackpot Junction:** Morton
S, B	⑨	**Lake of the Woods Casino:** Warroad
S, B	⑩	**Little Six Casino/Mystic Lake Casino:** Prior Lake
S, B	⑪	**Northern Lights Casino:** Walker
S, B	⑫	**The Palace Bingo & Casino:** Cass Lake
S, B	⑬	**Red Lake Casino:** Red Lake
S, B	⑭	**River Road Casino:** Thief River Falls
S, B	⑮	**Shooting Star Casino:** Mahnomen
S, B	⑯	**Treasure Island Casino:** Red Wing

S-Slot machines, **B**-Blackjack

Consequently, if you want to play the slots in Minnesota, you have to play a machine that duplicates reels on a video screen.

To some people, this is a big deal—or, more accurately, a "reel bad deal." After dozens of vacation trips to Las Vegas, the idea that you get the fairest shake from a spinning reel is strongly imprinted on some minds. But Minnesota adopted its video-game rule after deciding that computer chip-controlled video screens are more tamper-proof that devices that still employ some mechanical elements.

Like other states in the Midwest, the rules permitting slot machines specify a range of paybacks. A video gaming device must return no less than 80 percent for typical non-skill games, and no less than 83 percent for games where the player can affect the outcome—such as video poker. For video keno, the rules allow the casino to hold 25 percent.

Minnesota is unique because it also has limits on how much the gambling devices can pay out: No more than 95 percent for non-skill games and no more than 98 percent for games like video poker. As a result, you won't find what video-poker enthusiasts call a 9/6 poker machine, because its theoretical payout is more than 98 percent. Fortunately for Minnesota casinos, none of the other casinos in the Midwest have installed 9/6 machines.

Another development that relates to the video-slots rule is quickly apparent to any first-time Minnesota casino visitor. Casinos tend to have a big variety of video games—including video blackjack, eight-way match games, games with multiple betting on each line, games with multiple screens for jackpots and double-up features and games that don't even look like slot machines.

One is video craps, where six players crowd around a pair of giant upturned video screens that duplicate the "crapless craps" table that was invented in Las Vegas a number of years ago. Another is a video blackjack table, where players sit together around a semi-circular blackjack table facing a big TV dealer. Each player has his or her own TV monitor to hold the "cards" when they're dealt.

By 1995, industry insiders say Minnesota casinos will probably have a version of video roulette, assuming the systems are approved by state gaming authorities.

Indeed, to many first-time casino visitors, Minnesota gambling joints look suspiciously like video arcades. And that's part of the long-term picture, too. Most insiders think Minnesota's flirtation with casinos is a temporary thing and that survival has to be linked to the concept of resort destination. That means combining gambling with child-care facilities, entertainment complexes, hotels with pools and golf courses, RV and camping parks, and even more places to eat.

When you visit a Minnesota casino, expect to see some of these amenities. And if you visit again later, expect to see even more.

Black Bear Casino

Carlton, Minnesota
218-878-2327

Getting There: From Interstate 35, take the Highway 210 exit. The casino is visible from the interstate.

First Impression: Under the Big Top.

Overview: In June of 1993, the Fond du Lac Band of Chippewa closed their small reservation casino near Cloquet, Minn., and stepped into the big time with an 87,000-square-foot casino that's about 130 miles north of Minneapolis/St. Paul and about 25 miles south of Duluth. The round, domed casino was set close enough to I-35 so that casino officials could stand at the front door and hear the screech of brakes as tourist-filled cars exited the expressway and headed toward the Black Bear parking lot. The building is white faux-limestone, trimmed with colored panels in black, yellow and red, plus lots of neon. It's the first step in an ambitious building scheme that includes a retail shopping mall, hotel, gas station and American Indian interpretive center.

The Casino: Black Bear's two-story main rotunda is filled mostly with blackjack tables. Above the gamblers and dealers, the metal dome peaks to a high skylight. Interior features include a lot of tile and glass block, with slot parlors radiating from the main rotunda like spokes on a wheel. Escalators ferry patrons to the second floor, where there is a 500-seat bingo hall that doubles as the casino's lunch and dinner buffet. The facility has a sports bar with the requisite big-screen television, and the Lady Slipper Lounge, which features live music on weekends. This casino is big, but generally low-key—partly because of low blackjack betting limits ($200). Big crowds hit the casino on weekends, mostly coming from Duluth, and the summer vacation season brings in hordes of players, many from Canada and Wisconsin.

Hours: 24 daily.

In Play: 1,000 slot and video games (video poker, keno, blackjack, video craps), nickel to $1 machines. 24 blackjack tables ($2–$200), using six-deck shoes (three splits allowed, with double downs after splits; splitting aces requires one additional card). 500-seat bingo parlor features evening sessions.

Specials: Tuesday blackjack tournaments ($10 buy-ins, with reentries permitted). Club card.

Amenities: Liquor served in the gaming area. The Blackbear Lounge features a highly regarded walleye fish dinner, plus other entries in the $10–$12 price range.

Overnight: Construction on a resort hotel near the casino was expected to begin in the summer of 1994. Two close-by motels are the Americinn Motel of Carlton, $46–$51 (218-384-3535) and the Royal Pines Motel, $45 (218-384-4242). There's also an Americinn in Cloquet, about five miles away, $49–$66 (218-879-1231). Other lodging: the Driftwood Motel, $40–$50 (218-879-4638) and the Golden Gate Motel, $40–$50 (800-732-4241).

Other Reasons to Be Here: The Carlton-to-Duluth segment of the Willard Munger Trail provides incredible overviews of forest lands. Nearby Jay Cooke State Park features whitewater rafting, plus spectacular views of waterfalls along the St. Louis River. In Duluth, take the harbor cruise, tour the railroad museum, and stop at Hawk Ridge, one of the largest migratory flyways for hawks and eagles in North America.

Firefly Creek Casino

Granite Falls, Minnesota
612-564-2121

Getting There: From Granite Falls, take Highway 67 and drive five miles south to the casino.

First Impression: Down in the valley.

Overview: Firefly Creek was once viewed as the Minnesota casino most likely to go bankrupt. Though set in a pleasant valley along the Minnesota River in Southwestern Minnesota, the casino is in the state's rich prairie farming region—not exactly a destination hot spot. Worse, the little casino is less than a 40-minute drive from Jackpot Junction, one of the state's oldest gambling facilities and also one of its largest. But Firefly Creek has endured, and those who visit this region of the state also discover an area rich in history and natural beauty.

The Casino: The metal-sided building that houses the casino has a utility look to it. Inside, the casino's walls are decorated with Indian art and the small selection of games is attractively displayed. There's room enough for a progressive that has a car as a jackpot. The only source of food is a country-style cafe, complete with stools and tables, daily specials and home-style cooking. Locals often come here for coffee and pie. The formal dining room was converted into a lounge after the casino acquired a liquor license in 1994. Most of the casino visitors are regulars who know the staff and want what one called "that down-home feeling."

Hours: 24 hours on Fridays and Saturdays, 8 A.M. to 1 P.M. other days.

In Play: 350 slot and video games (video poker, keno, video blackjack). 10 blackjack tables ($2–$200), using four-deck shoes (four splits allowed, with double downs; one splitting of aces allowed, followed by a single card; dealer hits soft 17s).

Specials: Card club tracks play and rewards gamblers with merchandise.

Amenities: Country cafe. Gift shop. Liquor served in lounge.

Overnight: Try the Granite Falls Super 8 Motel, $43, which also has its own restaurant (612-564-4075). The budget-minded should try the Scenic Valley Motel, $32–$36 (612-564-4711).

Other Reasons to Be Here: The Yellow Medicine County Historical Museum has an interesting collection of pioneer and Indian artifacts, plus a display of exposed rocks that have been identified as the oldest in the world—some 3.8 billion years. The Riverside Collectors Society Gallery houses an extensive collection of art and gifts. The Upper Sioux Agency State Park, less than three miles from the casino, has a touch-and-see natural history interpretive center, plus 45 campsites, a boat landing and 18 miles of hiking trails. Local events include the Western Fest and Rodeo, held at the end of June.

Fond-du-Luth Casino

129 E. Superior St.
Duluth, Minnesota
800-873-0280
218-722-0280

Getting There: In downtown Duluth, on the city's main business street. Exit Interstate 35 at Fifth Avenue or Lake Avenue, then go east to Superior Street and turn north to the casino. The casino is on the corner of Superior Street and Second Avenue East.

First Impression: Minnesota's only downtown joint.

Overview: Fond-du-Luth, which is run by the Fond du Lac Band of Chippewa, came into being as the result of an agreement between the tribe and Duluth officials. The city ceded land containing an old commercial building in exchange for a partnership in casino profits. That agreement fell apart and the future of the casino is tied up in litigation. Meanwhile, the casino operates as a slot house and bingo parlor.

The Casino: The casino is housed in a restored, multi-story commercial building on Superior Street. Parking in an adjacent ramp is free, if you get your ticket validated. Inside, the main floor is reserved for slot machines and a small snack bar that serves grill food. The 525-seat bingo parlor is upstairs, and it's very popular with locals. Until the squabble is resolved with city officials, Fond-du-Luth is worth visiting only if you happen to be stuck in Duluth and love slot machines or bingo.

Hours: 24 Fridays through Sundays, 10 A.M. to 2 A.M. Mondays through Thursdays.

In Play: 400 slot and video keno machines, nickel to $1. Upstairs bingo hall has daily sessions.

Amenities: Snack bar. Free parking with validated ticket from adjacent parking ramp. Small lounge serving mixed drinks and beer.

Overnight: Like any big city, Duluth has plenty of places to stay. Fitger's Inn, a hotel housed in the old Fitger's Brewery building, is a unique alternative; it's next to the lake and part of a large indoor shopping mall and entertainment complex, $55–$105 (218-722-8826). Another upscale hotel is the Holiday Inn Duluth, 207 W. Superior St., which has 350 rooms and suites overlooking the harbor, $84–$195 (218-722-1202). For advice on a wide range of accommodations, call the Duluth Convention and Visitors Bureau (800-4-DULUTH).

Other Reasons to Be Here: For starters, drive across the Aerial Lift Bridge. Then, as your interest dictates, you can try the Canal Park Marine Museum, the Vista Cruise boat tours of the Lake Superior harbor, the historic Glensheen Mansion, the Depot Railroad Museum or tours of the land-locked William A. Irvin ore boat. Don't fail to steer your car along Skyline Drive, a dramatic three-mile road along the bluffs above the city, some 600 feet above the Lake Superior shoreline. Canal Park features a boardwalk that begins just a few short blocks away from the door of the casino and continues along the shore of the lake. If you decide to walk it, dress warm; Lake Superior is Duluth's natural air conditioner.

Fortune Bay Casino

Tower, Minnesota
800-992-7529
218-753-6400

Getting There: Take Highway 169 through Tower, turn left on Highway 77 and go two miles to Bois Fort Road, which leads to the casino. Many signs provide clear directions.

First Impression: Deep in the woods.

Overview: Of the smaller casinos in Minnesota, one of the most attractive is Fortune Bay, which is nestled in a splendid northern Minnesota forest of

Norway and jack pines near Lake Vermilion. This is a region that defines the state as a home to wolves and loons and quietly secluded cabins. It's also the "hard rock" region of Minnesota's Iron Range and any visit should include a stop at Tower Soudan Underground Mine State Park, where you can take a guided tour by riding a miner's elevator some 2,300 feet beneath the surface of the earth.

The Casino: Bingo halls aren't supposed to be beautiful, but Fortune Bay has created an exception. Its main, crescent-shaped hall is a cathedral for bingo, with a high central altar that houses lots of high-tech video equipment under a curved, pine-paneled ceiling. The main casino area, by contrast, is small, but handsomely laid out, with an elegant curved bar at one end of a fairly narrow, second-floor room. An addition was added in 1993, and a project started in 1994 will convert part of the big 750-seat bingo hall into an entertainment performing space. A casino-operated marina on Lake Vermilion opened in 1993, and a 105-room hotel is expected to open in 1995.

Hours: Noon to 1 A.M. Sundays through Thursdays; noon to 4 A.M. Fridays and Saturdays.

In Play: 260 slot and video games (video poker, keno, video blackjack), nickel to $1 machines. 16 blackjack tables ($2–100), using six-deck shoes (dealer hits on soft 17s; double downs after splits allowed, except split aces, which require one additional card). Bingo hall has evening sessions Wednesdays through Sundays, plus matinees on Saturdays and Sundays.

Specials: Regular promotions feature two-deck blackjack games. The card club, called the Wild Edge Club, qualifies active gamblers for double blackjack payoffs, casino-cash coupons, double payoffs on bingo and other specials.

Amenities: Liquor in gaming area. Small buffet restaurant serves lunches and dinners, plus breakfasts in summer. The house special: prime rib and crab legs, $9.50 on Mondays and Tuesdays.

Overnight: The Iron Range Convention and Visitors Bureau in Eveleth maintains a list of motels that have coupon and discount programs with the casino (800-777-8497 or 218-744-2441). Most short-term visitors stay in Virginia or Ely, though resorts on Lake Vermilion are among the finest in the state—and some of the most expensive, too.

Other Reasons to Be Here: Ely is the gateway to the Boundary Waters Canoe Area and the three-million-acre Superior National Forest, and it could double as a set for the TV show "Northern Exposure." The town, with its public sauna, has a rough-as-bark wilderness feel to it. Many backwoods pioneers pick up their monthly supplies here and get a bath, rubbing shoulders with city-dwelling vacationers who are getting ready for a canoe trip into the BWCA wilderness. The city's famous International Wolf Center features daylong, weekend and week-long adventures. In nearby Tower, stop at the Historical Museum, which is a fascinating place for railroad buffs.

Grand Casino Hinckley

Hinckley, Minnesota
800-472-6321

Getting There: One mile east of the Interstate 35 Hinckley exit on Highway 48.

First Impression: The ultimate emporium.

Overview: This casino has provided the financial muscle for Grand Casinos, Inc., a suburban Minneapolis-based company that is now operating big casino resorts in Mississippi and Las Vegas. The monster casino is part of a constantly growing resort development that is erupting out of a field near Hinckley. By the end of 1995, the complex is expected to include three hotels, an amphitheater, and an 18-hole golf course in addition to the 240-site RV park and 50-unit "chalet" development that is already operating. Most of the gambling crowds who patronize the casino come from the Minneapolis/St. Paul area, which is a quick 75-minute trip on I-35. In summer, the casino benefits from the many tourists who use the interstate to reach Minnesota's major wilderness areas near Lake Superior.

The Casino: Grand Casinos specialize in running gaming emporiums where everything is bright and cheerful, and filled with novelties. Some of the industry's newest devices are on display here—from video craps and electronic blackjack tables to a huge, theater-sized video bingo system that can cycle through four games of bingo in 30 seconds or less. In 1994, the casino built a new addition for its already-huge teen video arcade and Kid's Quest child-care center. The latter serves children between the ages of six weeks and 12 years and has equipment that any day care center would die for.

The complex seems to sprawl, but that's because the property is divided between reservation-owned land that belongs to the Mille Lacs Band of Chippewa, and non-reservation real estate that's controlled by Grand Casinos, Inc., the casino's management firm. A new hotel that opened in 1994 is owned by the management company—as is the Grand Grill Americana, a bar and restaurant that's connected to the casino by an enclosed corridor and is exempt from the tribe's severe restrictions on alcohol sales. Unlike the Grand Grill's bar, if you go to the Silver 7s Lounge in the casino, you have to abide by a strict two-drink limit. Drink prices at Grand Casino Hinckley include a 50-cent contribution to alcohol treatment programs.

Hours: 24 daily.

In Play: More than 1,500 slot and video games (video poker, keno, video blackjack, video bingo, video blackjack tables, video craps), nickel to $25 machines. 48 blackjack tables ($3–$1,000), using 6- and 8-deck shoes (double downs permitted after splits, except split aces, which require one additional card). Four video craps tables ($1 minimum bets). Eight video blackjack tables (quarter and $1 minimums, deck electronically shuffled between hands). Royal Ascot computerized horse-racing game.

Specials: Mega-jackpot slot games, including nickel progressives that start at $20,000, quarter progressives that start at $100,000 and $1 progressives that start at $250,000. Blackjack tournaments Wednesday evenings. "Baby" blackjack tournaments on Monday afternoons. Heavy coupon promotions. Grand Advantage players club rewards play with money and other perks. High-stakes gambling area.

Amenities: Kids Quest child-care center and video arcade. No-smoking areas. No alcohol in gaming area and alcohol consumption limited to two drinks at Silver 7s entertainment lounge. Free entertainment nightly. Grand buffet features 38 hot entries and received AAA rating as Minnesota's best buffet for two years in a row. Cherries snack bar provides deli items. Grand Grill Americana, connected by a walkway to the casino, has a specialty menu and is adjacent to the Carousel Bar, which is exempt from the casino's two-drink limit. Silver 7s Lounge also serves deli sandwiches. Bus and limo services can be booked through the casino. Headline entertainment in nearby amphitheater. An 18-hole golf course is scheduled to open in 1995.

Overnight: The Grand Hinckley Inn, located across the parking lot from the casino, is a 154-room luxury hotel that opened in May 1994. The hotel has an indoor pool and recreation complex, but no restaurant. A short shuttle ride from the casino is a 240-site RV park and chalet complex. The 50 identical mobile home-like chalets are neat little units, each with a comfortable living room, full kitchen and outdoor deck. Rates vary from $49 to $69, and there are frequent specials. The casino's main telephone number has a highly sophisticated message and transfer system for all services and it operates a "play-and-stay" program with many area hotels and resorts.

Other Reasons to Be Here: St. Croix State Park, the oldest and largest state park in Minnesota, is located east of the casino on Highway 48. The park has an extensive bicycle and hiking trail system, with gorgeous routes that meander along the scenic St. Croix River. The original town of Hinckley burned during a horrific fire storm in 1894 that killed hundreds of people; the town's main attraction is a fire museum, housed in a former railroad depot. On the way to the casino, stop at Toby's, located at the Hinckley interstate exit, and sample its famous caramel rolls.

Grand Casino Mille Lacs

Onamia, Minnesota
800-626-5825

Getting There: On Highway 169 between Onamia and Garrison on the southwest shore of Lake Mille Lacs.

First Impression: Nickel heaven.

Overview: Lake Mille Lacs is the center of the universe for serious walleye fishermen. At one time, the resorts that line the shores of the large lake were devoted almost exclusively to serving the fishing addicts who flock to the lake year-round. In winter, it's estimated that nearly 20,000 ice-fishing houses move onto the frozen lake, making it a good-sized city by Minnesota standards. In recent years, however, it's been possible to find tourists in the Mille Lacs area who don't fish (no kidding!). In summer, they come to play golf, to hike and to camp in the birch forests that ring the lake. Hunting is a major fall activity. In winter, snow activities—snowmobiling, cross-country skiing, snowshoe hiking—are popular. This is a prime outdoor tourist mecca.

The Casino: Dubbed the place for "walleye widows" and skunked fishermen when it opened in 1991, Grand Casino Mille Lacs is the smaller sibling of Grand Casino Hinckley, the other casino owned by the Mille Lacs Band of Chippewa. Both casinos have identical "resort destination" features— including on-site hotels, child-care facilities, big kid arcades and plenty of dining temptations. Both offer a glittering variety of gambling games. But Grand Casino Mille Lacs, unlike its twin, is totally alcohol-free and also has a big bingo program. It's also off the beaten path, with no interstate highways nearby. As a result, the casino has positioned itself as a haven for vacationing families and retired folks—people who have money, but don't plan to spend it all on gambling. The percentage of nickel slot machines here is huge, along with a bewildering variety of off-beat games. The atmosphere is like strolling through an amusement park.

Hours: 24 daily.

In Play: 1,200 slot and video games (video poker, keno, blackjack, video craps, video blackjack tables), nickel to $5 machines. 35 blackjack tables ($3–$1,000), using six- and eight-deck shoes (double downs after splits allowed, except for split aces, which receive one additional card). 400-seat bingo hall, with daily sessions except on Saturdays. Royal Ascot computerized horse-racing game.

Specials: Blackjack tournaments and other special gaming events are scheduled nearly every month. Heavy coupon promotions. Grand Advantage card club returns cash for play.

Amenities: No liquor. Some smoke-free areas. The equipment-packed Kids Quest child-care center takes children between six weeks and 12 years of age and is operated by New Horizons, one of Minnesota's biggest child-care chains. The nearby arcade has a huge variety of video games. The buffet is one of the biggest and best in the state. Other eating facilities include a full-service snack bar, called Plums, and the Grand Northern Grill, which serves traditional American dinners from a menu.

Overnight: An attached, 180-room hotel with a swimming pool and recreation area was scheduled to open in September 1994. Otherwise, the variety of lodges and motels in the area is huge, though reservations are advised in the summer months. The best-known lodge resort is Izatys Golf & Yacht Club, just east of Onamia, which has all the services and luxuries, $59–$319 (800-533-1728). The less-upscale Seguchie Resort, located between the casino and Garrison, offers casino packages and caters to the fishing and hiking crowd, $45–$65 (612-692-4140). For a bed-and-breakfast, try Cour du Lac, a secluded three-bedroom establishment near Onamia, $75–$95 (612-532-4627). Just south of Garrison, the Mille Lacs Motel has 15 knotty pine units overlooking the lake, $45–$55 (612-692-4349). Call the casino's main number to inquire about "play-and-stay" deals with local resorts and inns. And for additional information about lodging in the Mille Lacs area, call the Minnesota Office of Tourism: 800-657-3700.

Other Reasons to Be Here: The Native American museum, located just across the highway from the casino, provides a history of the Ojibwa people of Minnesota. Two state parks, Father Hennepin State Park and Kathio State Park, offer camping and miles of hiking trails. And, of course, there's always fishing.

Grand Portage Lodge & Casino

Grand Portage, Minnesota
800-543-1384 (hotel)
218-475-2441 (casino)

Getting There: Take Highway 61, also known as the North Shore Drive, to Grand Portage. The casino and lodge is at the south edge of the community, near the lake.

First Impression: Gambling is one small part.

Overview: When Indian gaming became legal in Minnesota, the Grand Portage Chippewa responded by utilizing existing convention space in their handsome Lake Superior resort. Unfortunately, the result was a fairly small, cramped, inadequately ventilated gaming hall. In 1994, a large new addition was built and the entire casino operation moved into it. The 100-room hotel, a former Radisson, is on the shore level of Lake Superior. The complex also includes a sheltered marina and an RV park that overlooks the bay.

The Casino: The lodge's new addition more than doubled the available space for gaming operations—and the change was long overdue. The casino is now one of the larger operations in the northern part of the state, and a majority of its patrons are Canadians. Bingo is played in a separate part of the lodge complex. Food services and other amenities remain tied to the lodge, which has a lovely lounge area that reminds visitors of the area's connection to the old days of the French fur traders. The casino tries to maintain its image as a "friendly little house," with low-limit tables and lots of nickels.

Hours: 24 daily.

In Play: 400 slot and video games (video poker, keno, blackjack, video craps), nickel to $1 machines. Eight blackjack tables ($2–$25), using six-deck shoes (three splits allowed, with double downs after splits; aces can be split once, requiring a single additional card). Video craps. Bingo sessions on Tuesday, Friday and Saturday evenings, plus Sunday matinees.

Specials: Blackjack tournaments begin in the fall of 1994. Casino officials plan to add a card club late in 1994 or early in 1995.

Amenities: The hotel operates a full bar; customers can carry drinks into the gaming area. The hotel's full-service restaurant has a reputation for outstanding lake trout dinners. A buffet is offered on Saturday nights.

Overnight: The lodge has 100 rooms, all with the same rate ($63 for two), plus an indoor pool and sauna. The North Shore region has many other well-known resorts, including the Lutsen Resort, $53–$225 (800-258-8736), and Crooked Lake Resort in Finland, Minn., $45–$100 (218-365-2124). To get a complete listing, call the Minnesota Office of Tourism (800-657-3700) or the state's regional office in Duluth (218-723-4692) and ask for the Northeastern guide and list of hotels.

Other Reasons to Be Here: The North Shore is the jewel of Minnesota's scenic areas, as well as a gateway to the Boundary Waters Canoe Area. The two-and-a-half-hour drive between Duluth and Grand Portage passes through a series of state parks (Cascade River, Gooseberry Falls, Split Rock and Temperance River). Major events at Grand Portage center around the voyageurs' rendezvous in August, which includes canoe races, ax throwing and other events at the Grand Portage National Monument. The community also is the mainland port for the ferry to Isle Royale National Park, some 20 miles offshore in Lake Superior. Grand Portage State Park boasts the state's highest waterfall.

Jackpot Junction

Morton, Minnesota
800-538-8379
507-644-3000

Getting There: From Minneapolis, take Highway 212 to Olivia, turn south on Highway 71 and follow the signs to the casino near Morton. From Interstate 90 take Highway 71 north to Redwood Falls, then take Highway 19 east to the casino.

First Impression: Big House on the Prairie.

Overview: It's ironic that Jackpot Junction is where an Indian casino first flourished in Minnesota, because the casino also is near the site where disaster struck the Indian nations more than a century ago. The Lower Sioux Agency, located about two miles down the road from the casino, is the place where a great war began on a warm August morning in 1862. That war raged on and off for nearly 30 years before ending with the slaughter of 300 starving Dakota Indians at Wounded Knee, S.D., in 1890. The Minnesota chapter of that war, called the Dakota Conflict, lasted just six weeks and it was followed by a forced exodus of the Sioux, or Dakota, tribes. That's why the Dakota reservations in Minnesota are so small. But if you take the time to look, the remnants of the past are everywhere in this region. You won't, however, find many references to the past at Jackpot Junction, where the emphasis is on gambling.

The Casino: Located about 100 miles southwest of Minneapolis/St. Paul, Jackpot Junction started as a bingo hall in 1984 and moved quickly into a casino operation a few years later. It's an out-of-the-way location, but the casino is one of Minnesota's biggest—the result of being the only major gambling joint in the state for so many years. To compete with newer, easier-to-reach casinos, Jackpot Junction advertises heavily, books lots of tour groups from far-away states, and offers low-cost transportation—including daily, round-trip commuter hops from its own bus station in the Minneapolis suburb of Eden Prairie. On weekends, the airport in nearby Redwood Falls is busy with commuter flights, including the casino's own low-cost shuttle from Minneapolis/St. Paul. If you don't arrive with some sort of discount coupon in your hand, it's likely that you'll receive something after you walk through the door. This is discount coupon heaven.

Many blackjack players like to come here because the house deals from two- and four-deck shoes and permits big betting. The casino also was one of the first in the state to serve liquor in the gaming areas and it routinely books big-name Nashville stars into its on-site theater. Cocktails are free in the high-stakes areas.

On the other hand, the casino isn't particularly pretty. It sprawls across several connected buildings, including a permanent inflated dome that houses a dining and entertainment venue. The main part of the building is a two-story structure that looks vaguely like an old-time saloon and hotel. The theme has faded under the force of many renovations. The upstairs area, with its balcony of wooden spindles, houses a high-stakes room called The Royal Depot.

Hours: 24 daily.

In Play: 1,200 slot and video games (video poker, keno, video blackjack, video blackjack tables, video craps), nickel to $25 machines. 63 blackjack tables ($2–$1,000), using two- and four-deck shoes (double downs permitted after splits except split aces, which require one additional card). Bingo hall seats 385 and offers two daily sessions (three on Sunday), including multi-state mega-bingo.

Specials: Information about discount coupons for food, transportation, free slot pulls, discounted concert tickets and "casino money" can be obtained from the casino Customer Service department. Using Jackpot Express transportation from Minneapolis/St. Paul usually includes gambling and food coupons, plus free drinks. The slot club, called The Express Club, rewards play with merchandise, tickets to concerts, free motel stays and other premiums. Blackjack tournaments are a regular feature.

Amenities: Three full-service bars. The full-service restaurant, Impressions, serves a traditional moderately-priced menu of steaks and chops and is considered one of the better eating establishments in the area. The Garden Court Buffet is located in a big inflated dome, which also houses some gaming operations and a performing venue. Bands and other entertainers perform nightly. Fast food can be bought at a cafeteria-style restaurant called The Full Deck.

Overnight: The casino operates a 90-site campground and RV park. Many of the local motels offer coupon packages and free shuttle service to the casino. The closest is Granite Valley Motel in Morton, $43 double (507-697-6205), which runs a 24-hour casino shuttle. Motel No. 71 is less than five minutes away, $33–$45 (800-437-4789). In Redwood Falls, alternatives include the Dakota Inn, $25–$50 (800-287-5443); the Redwood Inn, $25–$50 (800-801-3521);and the Super 8, $25–$50 (800-800-8000).

Other Reasons to Be Here: The casinos service center books three-hour bus tours of the area ($5) that include visits to the Lower Sioux Agency Interpretive Center, nearby St. Cornelia's Episcopal Church and the nearby Mdewakanton community trading post. The interpretive center is operated by the Minnesota Historical Society. From the center you can hike to the Redwood

Ferry Crossing, site of a major massacre during the Dakota Conflict. To the north, about a 10-minute drive, is the site where the 30-hour Battle of Birch Coolie took place. Farther east, at the ruins of Fort Ridgeley, visitors can see excavated building foundations and stop at another interpretive center during the summer. Redwood Falls is home to the Minnesota Inventors Museum (call 800-INVENT1), which shares quarters with the Redwood County Historical Society Museum. Gilwood Haven is a well-known art gallery, and just outside Redwood Falls is Gilfillan, a lavishly restored 1882 farmstead. Alexander Ramsey Park in Redwood Falls has been called the "Little Yellowstone of Minnesota." The 217-acre park encloses Ramsey Falls on the Redwood River, a zoo, playgrounds, campground and a nine-hole golf course.

Lake of the Woods Casino

1012 E. Lake St.
Warroad, Minnesota
218-386-3381

Getting There: Take Highway 11 to Warroad.

First Impression: Oui, Lac du Bois.

Overview: Warroad is the top of the world for Minnesotans, about 350 miles north and west of Minneapolis/St. Paul. The town of 1,700 is on the shore of Lake of the Woods, a remarkable, 90-mile-long lake with more than 14,000 islands—many of them home to hardy wilderness people who live by fishing. Warroad also serves as the administrative capital for residents of the Northwest Angle, a chunk of U.S. territory that is separated from Minnesota by the lake and a portion of Canada. For a remote region, the area around Warroad has an amazing number of year-round lodges and resorts. The casino, in fact, is part of a lakeside resort complex operated by the Red Lake Band of Chippewa.

The Casino: It's right on the shoreline, adjacent to a casino-affiliated hotel that has its own small marina. A restaurant belonging to the same complex is located about a half-block away. The casino is a small operation and nothing special, but it's the only game in town, with a loyal following.

Hours: 8 A.M. to 1 A.M. Sundays through Tuesdays, 24 hours Wednesdays through Saturdays.

In Play: 250 slot and video games (video poker, video keno). 10 blackjack tables ($2-$100), using four-deck shoes (double downs allowed after splits; splitting aces requires one additional card).

Amenities: Fishing tournaments sponsored by the casino include a big winter ice-fishing festival that attracts thousands of well-padded anglers. The casino is very busy in summer, more relaxed in winter. Coupons good for slot money are given to guests at local motels.

Overnight: The casino-affiliated Lake of the Woods Motel has 42 rooms and a small marina, $42 double (218-386-3381). The Patch Motel, across the street from the casino, has a pool and 80 rooms, $44 double (800-288-2753). The three-bedroom Hospital Bay Bed & Breakfast is a restored landmark on the Warroad River, about four blocks from the casino, $45 and up (800-568-6028 or 218-386-2627).

Other Reasons to Be Here: Zipple State Park is a 3,000-acre reserve filled with hiking trails and swimming facilities. Boats take visitors to nearby Massacre Island and Fort St. Charles. Fly-in fishing services are available everywhere; for more information call the Warroad Chamber of Commerce, 800-328-4455 or 218-386-3543.

Little Six Casino

Prior Lake, Minnesota
800-262-7799
612-445-6000 or 612-445-9000

Getting There: Near the Mystic Lake Entertainment Complex, about 20 miles south of Minneapolis/St. Paul. Take Interstate 35W through Burnsville to the Highway 42 exit. Go west on Highway 42 to Highway 83, and turn south to the casino. The Little Six entrance is north of the main entrance to the Mystic Lake complex.

First Impression: If you run it, they will come.

Overview: Little Six is the place where the massive Mystic Lake complex had its start, back in the days when Indian gaming consisted of high-stakes bingo. The site has since been converted into business and tribal offices, maintenance facilities and a tribal day-care center. But the old casino remains in operation, mostly for the patrons who have grown attached to the place over the years. The gaming area, however, is as large as some of Minnesota's smaller casinos.

The Casino: When slots were first introduced, the casino installed hundreds of machines that issued paper credits instead of coins, and they're still in use in the casino's main basement game room. An adjacent basement room in the "tepee" building has banks of newer machines, including many nickel slots. Low-stakes blackjack is played upstairs, in a little room near the Des Denah ("good food") cafe. A shuttle bus takes patrons to the Mystic Lake complex, about a half-mile away. Slot players crowd the area that has the newer, coin-spitting machines, but most avoid the old area, where there are lots of keno, poker and video blackjack machines that have poorer return rates.

Hours: 24 hours on weekends, 10 A.M. to 2 A.M. weekdays.

In Play: 470 slot and video games (video poker, keno, video blackjack), including many multi-game video units, mostly nickel to $1 machines. 10 blackjack tables ($3–$200), using four- to eight-deck shoes (double downs permitted after splits, except for split aces which receive one additional card).

Amenities: Small gift shop. Cafe-styled restaurant. No liquor. Regular shuttle bus to Mystic Lake complex.

Overnight: See the following listing for the Mystic Lake Entertainment Complex.

Mystic Lake
Entertainment Complex

Prior Lake, Minnesota
800-262-7799
612-445-6000

Getting There: 20 miles south of Minneapolis/St. Paul. From Interstate 35W in Burnsville, take County Highway 42 west to Highway 83. Turn south and go one mile to the complex. Alternative: From I-35W in Burnsville, take Highway 13 west, continuing when it becomes Highway 101. Turn south on Highway 83 and go five miles.

First Impression: Just like the Mall of America, sort of.

Overview: Mystic Lake is the biggest casino complex in the Midwest. Technically, it's three casinos, though two of them—Mystic Lake and the Dakota Country Casino—are merely (if that's the right word) giant sections of the same giant mall. The third casino, the Little Six, is in a separate building and gets a separate listing in this guide.

When it comes to huge casinos, presentation means a lot. In the case of Mystic Lake, you get an awesome view of the complex as you approach it from the hill on Highway 83. Seen at a distance, the two rounded gambling palaces and their connecting malls look like a huge, clean, high-tech industrial plant, surrounded by a square mile or so of parking lots. The parking lots are always full, but you can catch a shuttle bus from one of the parking-lot shelters and ride to one of the three main canopied entrances. On the other hand, this is one casino where paying for valet service makes sense.

The Mystic Lake entrance takes you directly into a Las Vegas–style casino, though the first thing you see is a fountain with a statue of an Indian maiden holding a water jar. The Dakota Country Casino has two entrances, one into the casino and the other into an enormous domed atrium that connects to a shopping mall and banquet halls—and to the casino, of course. One of the three main restaurants in the complex, the Minnehaha Cafe, is under the dome, sequestered by huge man-made boulders and a babbling little brook.

The Casinos: There are two casinos here because of a marketing need for diversity. Mystic, the original gambling hall, was a conscious effort to give local gamblers a big, upscale, Las Vegas-styled palace. Mystic's high-stakes blackjack area, where minimum bets reach the $100 range, is larger than the entire blackjack area in some smaller casinos. The rest of the circular gaming hall has that glitzy aura, with a sunken floor and a giant chandelier. Casino officials discovered that while many customers were delighted with the place, the upscale vastness of it made other patrons feel—well, common. So the Dakota Country Casino was built for the Middle-America folks, and to help handle the overwhelming crowds. As might be expected, the Dakota has a lot of low-end nickel machines, plus a huge collection of video poker machines in a section called "poker alley." Most of the casino's $3 blackjack tables are here, too. Overall, however, you won't find any gambling bargains.

And you won't find any liquor, either. The Mystic Lake complex is dry. There's a full-sized entertainment bar in the Dakota casino, called Wild Bill's Saloon, but it serves non-alcoholic cocktails and designer near-beers. Hint: German near-beer costs more and tastes worse than American near-beer.

The casino also has a no-smoking slot area with about 150 machines, plus no-smoking blackjack tables and no-smoking sections throughout the complex. And when they say no smoking, they mean it.

Nobody bends the rules at Mystic Lake. For obvious reasons, the management here has a very formal, almost paranoiac concern for rules and security. The video surveillance system is one of the best in the world and the security personnel think of themselves as a quasi-police force. In several celebrated cases, bank robbers were arrested after Mystic Lake security cameras tracked their spending habits with ill-gotten loot.

The casino was the first to hire an outside firm to help with counseling on gambling addiction and it has become a major contributor to many charitable causes. For most people, all this is a comfort. For others, the antiseptic quality of the casino operation feels a bit weird, especially since it is a haven for high-rollers.

Hours: 24 daily.

In Play: 2,100 slot and video games (video poker, video keno, video black-jack, video craps, and other video games), nickel to $25 machines. 128 blackjack tables ($3–$1,000), using four- to eight-deck shoes, depending on table minimums. 1,200-seat bingo palace has daily matinee and evening sessions, using recycled bingo sheets.

Specials: Monthly blackjack and slot tournaments are planned for 1994. A card club, called The Preferred Players Club, will be introduced in 1994 or 1995. The bingo hall participates in the multi-state mega-bingo system, where the grand prize is at least $1 million.

Amenities: There are a lot of reasons for the non-gambler to go to Mystic Lake. Let's start with the principal one: eating. The casino's buffet, the Four Seasons, is more like an upscale restaurant than a mass-feeding place, and the food is consistently top-rated. The $8.95 dinner price is a little higher than some buffets; Wednesday is seafood night for $11.95. The High Steaks Ranch House (get the pun?) sits in the Dakota gaming area and specializes in charred meats. The Minnehaha Cafe has lighter fare and is preferred by many because of its airy, atrium surroundings. There's also a big-selection deli, a concession stand in the bingo hall and espresso and snack carts in the shopping-mall corridors.

Which brings us to shopping. The Mall at Mystic Lake has nine retail shops. All are businesses operated by Native Americans, specializing in crafts and arts, plus a beauty salon, a novelty photo store and the usual reservation smoke shop. Most of these shops are designer places, with upscale prices. But you won't find a lot of the merchandise elsewhere.

For entertainment, the stage at Wild Bill's Saloon features country bands every night. Headliners perform in what the casino euphemistically calls its Celebrity Palace. Actually, the handsome, tiered bingo hall can be converted into a performance venue seating 2,460 paying customers. Other acts occasionally perform in the convention halls near the shopping areas.

Overnight: Casino officials dream of building a major high-rise hotel near the casino within the next few years, though nothing has been announced. For the time being, the closest hotel is the Canterbury Inn, five miles north of the casino on Highway 83. Canterbury has two restaurants and an enclosed atrium with pool and hot tub; rooms range from singles for $72 to two-room suites for $89–$119 (800-528-1234 or 612-445-3644). In 1994, Mystic Lake opened an RV park near the casino.

Other Reasons to Be Here: The twin cities of Minneapolis and St. Paul, with dozens of museums, nearly 100 theaters, two zoos, sports teams, beautiful parks, urban blight and suburban sprawl.

Northern Lights Casino

Walker, Minnesota
~~97.60~~ 800-252-7529
218-547-2744

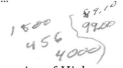

Getting There: Four miles south of Walker, at the junction of Highways 371 and 200.

First Impression: A stop and shop.

Overview: The Northern Lights and Palace casinos are less than 30 miles apart, both run by the Leech Lake Band of Chippewa. The idea is to divide the market. The Palace is a party and bingo place with no booze. Northern Lights, by contrast, is more of a business-like casino, serving liquor. Northern Lights is not as nice-looking as the Palace, but it is in a well-traveled location and it's surrounded by tourist businesses. Plans to expand the casino into a major resort have been on hold for some time.

The Casino: Situated beside the highway, Northern Lights looks like a converted Kmart. Inside, however, it has a 360-degree bar surrounded by slot machines. The place feels cramped, though a recent addition in the back added an entertainment area and more slot machines. The casino has a solid, if somewhat stolid, clientele, plus lots of summer tourists. Blackjack is popular here, and there is a lot of tournament play.

Hours: 24 daily.

In Play: 700 slot and video games (video poker, keno, video blackjack), nickel to $1 machines. 12 blackjack tables ($3–$200), using six-deck shoes (dealer hits on soft 17s; double downs after splits allowed, except aces which require one additional card).

Specials: Blackjack tournaments every week. Mini-blackjack tournaments Monday through Thursday.

Amenities: 24-hour, full-service restaurant and buffet specializes in prime rib. Liquor served. Summer outdoor festivals include a Country Fest in July and a Cajun Fest in August.

Overnight: Contact the Leech Lake Area Chamber of Commerce for a complete list of the many resorts and lodges in the area (800-833-1118 or 218-547-1313). The Inn at the Y is located across the highway from the casino, $39–$43 double (800-279-5373). Other Walker motels include an Americinn, $49–$55 (800-634-3444); the Lakeview Inn, $34–$55 (800-252-5073) and the Northwood Beach Resort Motel, $40–$65 (218-547-1702).

Other Reasons to Be Here: Walker bustles with quaint shops, restaurants, and, of course, fishing guide services. The Leech Lake Sailing Regatta takes place here every summer. Walker also hosts the International Eel Pout Fishing Contest in winter (an eel pout looks exactly the way its name suggests). The Heartland Trail, extending from Park Rapids to Walker, places bike riders in some of the most beautiful country in the region. Visit the Cass County Historical Museum to see logging and Ojibwe memorabilia.

Palace Bingo & Casino

Cass Lake, Minnesota
800-228-6676
218-335-6787

Getting There: Two miles west of Cass Lake on Highway 2. Turn north on Bingo Palace Drive and go one mile to the casino.

First Impression: A Greco-Tahitian spa, with neon trim.

Overview: Small can be classy, a fact demonstrated by the Palace Casino, which is situated on the Leech Lake Reservation about 15 miles east of Bemidji. This is deep timber country, the mythical home of Paul Bunyan. Almost everyone who comes here visits Itasca State Park, just south of Bemidji, where they wade across the ankle-deep headwaters of the Mississippi River and see the state's largest white and red pines. The casino is deep on reservation land, near a big athletic field and next to the site for summer powwows.

The Casino: The Palace bills itself as Minnesota's first fully themed casino. And that theme is . . . tropical paradise, sort of. Somehow, the designers managed to blend Greek columns with thatch huts and leaded colored windows to produce a pleasing melange that suggests somewhere warm and breezy. Even the neon is pastel. Luaus usually take place in the winter.

The casino provides the regional headquarters for big-time bingo. About half of the building is reserved for the 700-seat parlor, which even includes a 200-seat no-smoking area. But unlike a lot of bingo halls, where all the business is serious, bingo at the Palace sometimes gets pretty frivolous—especially when the management hosts weird prize drawings or engages in a local favorite: a wheel-spinning game called Let's Make a Treaty. The tropical part of the casino also has a full-service restaurant and a small community room, where dances and stage shows are scheduled every other weekend. Best winter deal: the weekend barbecue buffet, which costs $6.95, but includes a coupon worth $5 in casino money.

Hours: 24 daily.

In Play: 400 slot and video games (video poker, keno, video blackjack), nickel to $1 machines. 12 blackjack tables ($3–$200), using six-deck shoes (dealer hits on soft 17s; double downs permitted after splits, except for split aces, which require one additional card). Bingo sessions nightly except Tuesdays. Matinees on Sundays. Mega-bingo offered.

Specials: Coupon and promotional specials and jackpots offered throughout the year. Blackjack tournaments every Tuesday ($20 buy-in), plus special holiday tournaments throughout the year.

Amenities: The Palace Garden, a full-service restaurant, specializes in prime rib ($7) and walleye fish. Summer activities include frequent specials, such as a Mexican Fest, and "Around the World" dinner shows. Entertainment headlined about twice each month. No liquor.

Overnight: Big resorts can be found in this region. For information, call the Cass Lake Area Civic and Commerce (800-356-8615 or 218-335-6723) or the Bemidji Area Chamber of Commerce (800-458-2223 or 218-751-3541). In Bemidji, overnight visitors can try the Americinn Motel, $56–$59 (800-634-3444); the Paul Bunyan Motel, $24–$72 (800-848-3788) or the Royal Motel, $34–$50 (800-456-5443). In Cass Lake, the Whispering Pines Motel caters to hunters and fishermen, $31–$33 (218-335-8852).

Other Reasons to Be Here: Visitors are required (well, not really) to visit the big concrete statues of Paul Bunyan and Babe the Blue Ox, standing 18 feet tall in Bemidji's Lakeside Park. While there, take the kids on some rides at the amusement park, or tour the lake in the ferry boat. The Paul Bunyan Trail extends from Bemidji to Brainerd and is used by skiers, hikers and smowmobilers. The Paul Bunyan Playhouse in Bemidji is the oldest professional summer stock theater in Minnesota.

Red Lake Casino

Red Lake, Minnesota
218-679-2500

Getting There: 26 miles north of Bemidji on Highway 89, then turn right on Highway 1 and go about one mile to the casino.

First Impression: Minnesota's smallest.

Overview: Red Lake is one of the most remote areas in Minnesota and its vast wilderness quality is appealing to many. Hunting and fishing are major activities here, along with the big woods of northern Minnesota. The community is situated on Lower Red Lake, a reservation-only fishing lake.

The Casino: The Red Lake Band of Chippewa maintain this casino primarily for tribal customers. The casinos in Warroad and Thief River Falls are the tribe's principal money-makers. This, on the other hand, is the equivalent of a convenience store, though it's a friendly little place.

Hours: 10:30 A.M. until empty, usually 1 or 2 A.M. at the latest.

In Play: 86 slot and video games (video poker, keno), mostly nickel and quarter machines. Three blackjack tables ($2–$25) using four- or six-deck shoes.

Amenities: Concession stand serving grill food. No liquor.

River Road Casino

Thief River Falls, Minnesota
218-681-4062

Getting There: Six miles south of Thief River Falls. From Highway 59, take Pennington County Road 3 east to the casino.

First Impression: Fits the landscape.

Overview: This area of northwest Minnesota is flat and stoic, vast and panoramically beautiful. It's farm country, the prairie broken by the occasional grain elevator that rises from a small dusty town like a skyscraper. The little River Road Casino fits the landscape of pole barns and other rough buildings, and its staff expects customers to be just as polite as they are. If you ask about a place to stay, don't be surprised if a casino employee volunteers to call all the motels in the area to find an available room.

The Casino: River Road is a comfortable, clean, boring little place. The casino gets a fair share of customers from Grand Forks, N.D., who travel about 60 miles each way, plus lots of locals who don't care for the flashy atmosphere and alcohol consumption at the big Shooting Star complex in Mahnomen, about 60 miles to the south. Inside, the casino's one-story rectangular hall is decorated with paintings by Indian artists and the usual assortment of stuffed deer heads and record walleye fish.

Hours: 24 hours Wednesdays through Sundays, 8:30 A.M. to 1 A.M. Mondays and Tuesdays.

In Play: 250 slot and video games (video poker, keno), nickel to $5 machines. 10 blackjack tables ($2–$100, higher limits possible), using six-deck shoes (double downs permitted after splits, except for split aces which receive one additional card). The bingo hall seats 200 and schedules evening sessions Wednesdays through Sundays.

Amenities: Snack bar offers dinner specials. No alcohol.

Overnight: The Best Western in Thief River Falls offers casino coupons and has a pool and restaurant, $32–$64 (800-528-1234 or 218-681-7555). The C'mon Inn, which has similar amenities, also is recommended by locals, $40–$75 (800-950-8111 or 218-681-3000). Other lodging in Thief River Falls includes the Hartwood Motel, $27–34 (218-681-2640); the Super 8 Motel, $39–$43, (800-800-8000) and the T-59 Motel, $25–$45 (800-951-5959 or 218-681-2720).

Other Reasons to Be Here: The Agassiz National Wildlife Refuge is the only refuge in the Lower 48 states that has a resident wolf pack. It's unlikely that you'll spot any wolves on the 61,000 acres that the refuge shares with the Thief Lake Wildlife Management Area, but you may see deer, moose, elk and bear. You can also visit the Friendship Garden and Pioneer Village in Thief River Falls. In winter, the fact that the city is corporate headquarters for Arctic Cat may have something to do with the 400 groomed snowmobile trails in the area.

Shooting Star Casino

Mahnomen, Minnesota
218-935-2701
800-453-7827 (hotel only)

Getting There: In Mahnomen, about 35 miles north of Detroit Lakes and 60 miles south of Thief River Falls on Highway 59.

First Impression: Why here? Why not?

Overview: Mahnomen is a dusty prairie town on the far western edge of Minnesota. Once a blink in the flat landscape, it has become the home of the Shooting Star Casino resort, right down the highway from the Farmers Coop Elevator. Conventional wisdom says this is a crazy place for a giant casino—let alone a spanking-clean casino with a 244-room resort hotel and a big showroom that headlines Nashville stars every month. But they built it, and the people come. What they find is a complete resort—from swimming pools to an upscale Italian restaurant, from nightly entertainment to a kids' arcade. Because of its location, Shooting Star was the first Minnesota casino to represent itself as a complete getaway destination. And it has worked.

The Casino: Shooting Star is a very pleasant place to spend your time and money. The gambling area has a nice open feeling that results from a high-peaked ceiling with skylights. One of the nicest features is the Mustang Lounge, a sunken, clamshell bar that has a bandstand above it. It's right in the gaming area, but the noise (usually musical noise) is not distracting.

The games here are fairly conventional, though you can play a version of blackjack on one of the multi-game video machines. Table blackjack tends to be low-end; dealers hit on soft 17s to increase the house edge. Bingo is played in an old building on the other side of the huge parking lot.

Hours: 24 daily.

In Play: 900 slot and video games (video poker, keno), nickel to $1 machines. 32 blackjack tables ($3–$100), using six-deck shoes (dealer hits on soft 17s; double downs after splits permitted, except for split aces which take one additional card). Nightly bingo sessions in separate bingo hall.

Specials: Blackjack tournaments on Tuesday evenings ($20 buy-in). Frequent promotional specials and coupon offerings.

Amenities: A 1993 expansion added a terrific new atrium with an indoor pool, sauna and hot tub, plus a tropical bar and pool-side deli. A cabaret showroom features big-name Nashville stage shows several times a month. Free entertainment is provided most nights at the Mustang Lounge. A buffet restaurant serves most of the casino customers, but more discriminating eaters should check out Casa Roma, a wonderfully secluded Italian restaurant on the premises that serves with discreet formality. The teen arcade in the basement of the hotel is nothing special, but additional amusements for children, plus a child-care facility, are planned as part of an upcoming building phase.

The casino's need to attract customers from afar has resulted in some attractive tour and weekend packages. If planning a trip, call to check on special deals.

Overnight: The casino's attached hotel has regular-sized rooms, plus huge suites for high-rollers and willing-to-pay guests. The layout of the complex makes it possible to keep children away from the gambling operation, $52–$62 (800-453-7827). The Stardust Suites, located just across from the casino, is a new, 57-room motel; rates include a continental breakfast and free plug-ins for your car in winter, $50–$75 (218-935-2761).

Other Reasons to Be Here: That's a problem, unless you like the prairie (and a lot of people do). A drive east brings you to the White Earth State Forest and, if you travel more than 50 miles, to Minnesota's central resort/fishing areas. Fargo and Grand Forks are 60 to 75 miles away in North Dakota, and both have entertainment and shopping districts. For the most part, if you're planning to go to Shooting Star, plan on hanging out once you arrive. The casino has done its best to give you reasons to stay.

Treasure Island Casino

Red Wing, Minnesota
800-222-7077

Getting There: About 35 miles south of St. Paul and eight miles north of Red Wing. Take Highway 61 and follow the signs to the casino, which is in the Minnesota River Valley.

First Impression: Rooms with no view.

Overview: The area between Hastings and Red Wing is part of the Great River Road, which traces a scenic excursion through historic Mississippi River towns from Bemidji, Minn., to the Gulf of Mexico. To get to the casino, you drop down over the river bluffs and skirt along the flood plain, taking a new access road that was built to help handle the crowds. Treasure Island is one of two "metro" casinos in Minnesota—the other is Mystic Lake—and it is always crowded with gamblers from Minneapolis/St. Paul. The casino began in 1984 as the Prairie Island Bingo Hall, and big square casino rooms were tacked on as the business expanded. The result wasn't aesthetically pleasing until a new atrium and entertainment section was added in 1993.

Since then, the casino has worked hard on the amenities—even though management roulette and legal squabbles seem endemic to the place. The casino books stand-up comics and other name acts every week as free entertainment. It also brings in big-name bands several times a month for weekend gigs. Ground breaking for a new resort hotel took place in 1993, though the project remained stalled for many months. The casino has an RV park and a marina on the Mississippi, plus a community day-care center that can be used by visitors.

The Casino: Treasure Island's main gambling area is a series of large, square rooms, with blackjack tables in the center and slots around the perimeter. From the outside, the place looks like a pink-colored factory. If you go to the canopied entrance, however, you find yourself in a lovely domed atrium with palm trees. Toucan Harry's bar has been built to look like it's been placed in the bow of a wrecked pirate ship. The open feeling of the atrium soon disappears as you enter the gaming rooms, where you're always confronted by crowds of people.

Treasure Island pushes promotional gimmicks, and there's some kind of special event or jackpot nearly every day—from bonus coins and double jackpots to extra points in the Captain's Club slot club. The last room is the original, 500-seat bingo hall, which was remodeled in 1994. The casino is a favorite haunt for serious blackjack players from Minneapolis/St. Paul. That's because it's possible to play at tables with low-deck shoes without having to make sky-high wagers; the cut card can be placed way back in the shoe; and the casino seems more tolerant of card counters. For certain customers, the casino has been known to take bets up to $2,000, though you never see that high a limit on any of the tables in the high-stakes room.

Hours: 24 daily.

In Play: 1,250 slot and video games (video poker, keno, video blackjack, video craps), nickel to $5 machines. 52 blackjack tables ($3–$500), using shoes holding from two to six decks, depending on minimum bets (double downs allowed after splits, except for split aces, which require one additional card). Bingo hall has daily matinee and evening sessions.

Specials: Slot tournaments planned. Blackjack tournaments on Thursday evenings, plus red-eye blackjack tournaments at 1:30 A.M. Tuesdays. Special promotional events take place throughout the year.

Amenities: Child care is provided at the Children's Center of Prairie Island, located across the road from the casino, from 9 A.M. to 11 A.M. every day. Reservations required: 800-554-5473 or 612-385-0351. Standup comedians perform every Tuesday night; there's no admission charge or reservations for the two shows. Bands, big-screen boxing, stage shows and other entertainers are regular features. Joining the Captain's Club puts you on the mailing list for glossy brochures and plenty of coupons.

Liquor is served in the casino and at Toucan Harry's Bar. The buffet serves from 7 A.M. to 11 A.M. ($3.95 breakfast, $5.95 lunch, $7.95 dinner) and features prime rib on Saturday for $9.95. Fast food is available from snack bars in the bingo hall and casino.

Overnight: The historic St. James Hotel in downtown Red Wing has huge, superbly renovated rooms that are filled with antiques, $95–$145 (800-252-1875). The Red Carpet Inn is adjacent to the Pottery Place shopping mall, $51–$63 (800-251-1962). The Quiet House Suites specializes in amenities that include private balconies, whirlpools for two, theme rooms, and a swim-through indoor/outdoor pool; rates vary according to services (800-528-1234). Call the Red Wing Chamber of Commerce for information about the many bed-and-breakfast inns in the area (800-762-9516).

Other Reasons to Be Here: Known throughout the country for Red Wing Shoes and Red Wing stoneware, the historic town of Red Wing is a favorite destination for Minneapolis/St. Paul residents and tourists. There are two ski resorts in the area—at Frontenac and Welch—plus many opportunities for hiking, cycling and canoeing. Many people come here to shop, however. The old stoneware factory has been turned into the Pottery Place Shopping Mall, a collection of interesting stores. Downtown, the St. James Shopping Court draws other shoppers to its enclosed mall. In summer, take a tour of Lake Pepin on an excursion boat that docks just below the St. James Hotel. Several parks on the bluffs in the city provide panoramic views of the Mississippi.

CHAPTER 5

NORTH DAKOTA

The Rules of the Game: Casino gaming came to North Dakota in 1993, but gambling is nothing new in the Flickertail State. Since the late 1970s, the state's charitable gambling law has allowed blackjack, pull-tabs, bingo, race betting and "paddle wheels." The latter is a crude version of roulette, using an elaborate betting table and a vertical, wheel-of-fortune type of spinner.

Blackjack is played at more than 300 sites and pull-tabs are even more common, sold from "tip jars" or from machines. Bingo parlors are endemic. Paddle wheels, which sucked up money faster than a prairie tornado, have almost disappeared—proving that you can't fool even some of the people all of the time.

Charitable gaming has produced some strange bedfellows. The biggest non-Indian gaming operation in the state, for example, is operated by Prairie Public Television, which did $10 million in business in 1993 from 10 different locations. The Teamsters union operates the nation's highest-grossing pull-tab site in Fargo, where an average of $14,500 in pull-tabs were sold every day during 1993.

When the first Indian casino opened in December 1992, the initial rush came from folks who wanted to try out that new contraption: the slot machine. Single payline, reel-type slots are still the dominant games, generally played by dogged nickel and quarter bettors. Some of the smaller casinos have not yet introduced video poker machines and there's no great rush to play video poker at the casinos that have them.

The state has negotiated five gaming compacts with Indian groups. The compacts allow slots, video games, blackjack, poker, keno, craps and a local game called "Indian dice." Games covered under charitable gambling also are allowed in casinos, and the door is open for agreements to allow sports and calcutta pools and parimutuel and simulcast operations.

Pre-casino gambling laws placed tight betting limits on the charitable games—including a $5 limit on blackjack. The compacts covering casinos are only slightly looser. In blackjack, for instance, casinos can accept bets up to $50.

The compacts also set overall payback limits for slot machines at no less than 80 percent and no more than 100 percent for non-skill games, and between 83 and 100 percent for skill games, such as video poker. Late in 1993, a survey by state gaming officials determined that slots were returning an average of about 91.6 percent overall. The range was from 84.7 percent for some non-skill nickel progressives to 97.4 percent for some poker machines.

Under a separate compact, the state's largest casino—Prairie Knights near Bismarck—has a $5 limit on slot machines. Slots at other casinos can accept three simultaneous bets of $5 each. These restrictions aren't all that significant for slot games, but they may prove tricky for video craps, video blackjack and other high-tech games that accept multiple bets.

For poker, the compacts limit bets to $10 per round, with a three-round maximum. Prairie Knights' separate compact provides for a $25 single bet and $50 overall, but the casino allows five-round, $10 bets. The rake at all casinos is 10 percent, up to a maximum of $3 per pot.

Craps is being introduced, but slowly. Early in 1994, only one casino—the Dakotah Sioux near Devils Lake—was operating a craps table, although Prairie Knights and 4 Bears casinos had space set aside for a single table in each casino. The compact limits bets to $25 overall, though it appears that the rule will be bent or modified.

The Name of the Game: North Dakota has been carved rather nicely into four major casino districts—North, Central, West and South. What could be called "second-generation" casinos opened late in 1993 at 4 Bears in New Town and at Prairie Knights in Cannon Ball. These are upscale operations, with nice facilities, snazzy restaurants, flashy bars and entertainment venues. The casinos at Belcourt and Devils Lake, by contrast, are first-generation, small-town operations.

Improvements are anticipated—including a big resort hotel at Prairie Knights Casino and perhaps an entirely new facility to replace the two little casinos near Devils Lake. But it's unlikely that the overall number of casinos in North Dakota will increase, according to state gaming authorities.

Dakotah Sioux Casino

St. Michael, North Dakota
701-766-4866

Getting There: Eight miles south of Devils Lake on Highway 57. Take Highway 20 south from Devils Lake and look for the Highway 57 turnoff.

First Impression: Bingo-land.

The Casino: This is a rundown bingo hall and slot joint for the locals. It opened in December of 1992 as North Dakota's first casino—and it remains an inadvertent symbol of how far the state's Native American gaming industry has progressed. The bingo hall is an old school gymnasium. Two small connecting rooms were turned into slot parlors, and what looks like a prefab building was added to house more machines. The latter is connected to the old gym by a ramp that's steep enough to strike terror in the hearts of most senior citizens. The slots are dominated by nickel and quarter machines, including low-yielding video poker machines.

Hours: 24 daily.

In Play: 102 slots and video poker games, nickel to $1, including progressives. Big bingo hall offering daily sessions.

Amenities: Snack counter, plenty of help-yourself free coffee. No liquor. For other information, see the following description of the Dakotah Sioux Casino at Tokio.

Dakotah Sioux Casino

Tokio, North Dakota
701-294-2109

Getting There: 18 miles south of Devils Lake on Highway 20. Watch for the hand-painted casino signs.

First Impression: This is only temporary, isn't it?

Overview: Devils Lake is actually a chain of natural lakes that are popular with waterfowl hunters and fisher-persons. The prairie community of about 7,500 is on the north side of the chain. It still has a vibrant downtown business district, housed in vintage, two-story brick buildings. Don't be put off by the outskirts' unattractive clutter of motels, car dealerships and truck stops. In the winter, the parking lots at movie theaters, bars and restaurants are full of unlocked cars, all with their motors running. When a car gets stolen, people talk about it for days. Nearest city: Grand Forks, N.D., 90 miles east.

The Casino: This is the larger of two small casinos operated in tribal villages by the Devils Lake Band of Sioux. The other is a bingo hall and slot joint, located about eight miles away in St. Michael (see previous listing). A proposal to build an upscale casino on the outskirts of Devils Lake has been

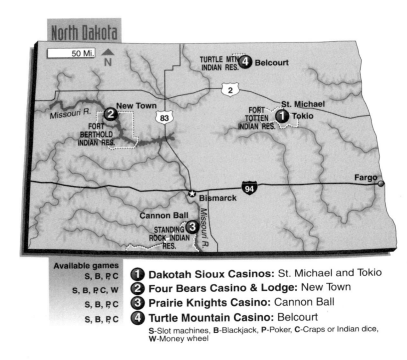

50 Mi.
N

TURTLE MTN. ❹ Belcourt
INDIAN RES.

2

New Town
Missouri R.
❷
FORT
BERTHOLD
INDIAN RES.

83

FORT
TOTTEN
INDIAN RES.

St. Michael
❶ Tokio

Fargo

★ Bismarck

94

Cannon Ball
STANDING ❸
ROCK INDIAN
RES.

Missouri R.

Available games

S, B, P, C	❶	**Dakotah Sioux Casinos:** St. Michael and Tokio
S, B, P, C, W	❷	**Four Bears Casino & Lodge:** New Town
S, B, P, C	❸	**Prairie Knights Casino:** Cannon Ball
S, B, P, C	❹	**Turtle Mountain Casino:** Belcourt

S-Slot machines, **B**-Blackjack, **P**-Poker, **C**-Craps or Indian dice, **W**-Money wheel

delayed by a lawsuit involving reservation boundaries. The present casino is a frequently overcrowded former school gymnasium, a concrete block building that has been painted blue and topped with a satellite TV monitor. It houses the games, and little else. The employees, however, offer plenty of genuine hospitality.

Hours: 24 daily.

In Play: 238 slots and video games (video poker, keno), nickel to one-coin $5 machines, including progressives; seven blackjack tables ($2–$50) using six-deck shoes; two craps tables ($2–$25); five poker tables ($1–$10) offering stud, high-low and straight-high, plus Texas Hold 'Em. Craps and poker tables are usually operating only in the evening.

Specials: Poker tournaments every other Sunday. Daily drawings, plus frequent cash coupon redemption programs. Poker "Shoot-Out" tournament on Thursdays ($25 buy-in, $650 total prizes). "Tropical Tuesday" blackjack tournaments in the winter feature travel prizes to warm places. Monday is senior citizen day.

Amenities: Separate cafeteria-style cafe offers daily specials, often with sides like mashed potatoes and peas. Continental breakfasts daily. No liquor.

Overnight: There's nothing nearby—repeat, nothing. The Artclare, on Highway 2 east of Devils Lake, is a full-service lodge, with pool, coffee shop, dining room and a lounge that offers $5-limit blackjack and off-track simulcast horse racing. Rates are $16.95–$24.95 single and $24.95–$32.95 double (701-662-4001). Other lodging: Comfort Inn, Devils Lake (701-662-6760); Days Inn, Devils Lake (701-662-5381).

Restaurants: Felix's in Devils Lake, an ersatz Tudor dining establishment, features steaks, prime rib and a full bar; Mr. and Mrs. J's in Devils Lake is a cafe featuring a 70-item salad bar and a 12-egg breakfast omelet, appropriately named "The Pig-Out."

Other Reasons to Be Here: The Fort Totten State Historic Site is a nineteenth-century outdoor museum that includes 16 of the original 39 buildings that served first as a military post and later as an Indian school. Fort Totten Days in late July feature the North American Indian Dancing Competition and a rodeo. The North Dakota Roughrider Rodeo Finals also are held here in the fall. Sully's Hill National Wildlife Preserve, about one mile east of Fort Totten, is one of four refuges in the United States for American bison and elk. And there's always fishing.

4 Bears Casino and Lodge

New Town, North Dakota
800-294-5454

Getting There: Four miles west of New Town on Highway 23.

First Impression: There's hope for North Dakota.

Overview: New Town is a fairly typical western Dakota community. The simple one- and two-story buildings have a hard, weathered appearance, and so do many of the people. Nearby, the vast, flat Dakota prairie gives way to rounded foothills above the Missouri River, which has been transformed into Lake Sakakawea by the Garrison Dam project. Fishing resorts are everywhere. Local boosters like to brag about the nine-hole golf course, which has real grass greens; $9 lets you play all day.

Nearest cities: Williston, 70 miles west; Bismarck, 150 miles southeast.

The Casino: 4 Bears began when a small casino was added to an existing, 40-room lodge that was situated on a spectacularly scenic hill overlooking a long, narrow bridge that crosses the Missouri River. A 22,000-square-foot addition received its grand opening in January 1994, and construction began immediately on a hotel expansion (to 80 rooms) and a 7,800-square-foot bingo hall. Wisely, the casino designers opted for higher ceilings, wider aisles and a sense of class. There's nothing awe-inspiring about this casino, but gamblers will find it a comfortable place to hang out.

Hours: Opens at 10 A.M. daily. Closes at 2 A.M. Sundays through Thursdays, 4 A.M. Fridays and Saturdays.

In Play: 392 slots and video games (video poker, keno), nickel to one-coin $5 machines; four progressives. 14 blackjack tables ($2-$50), using six-deck shoes (dealer hits on soft 17s; two splits are allowed, but no one-card rule for splitting aces; possible to double down after all splits). One craps table ($50 limit) with a standard Atlantic City layout. One money wheel. Poker room with four tables ($50 total bet limit per pot), offering stud, Texas Hold 'Em and high-low. Large, 336-seat bingo hall.

Specials: Slow-day tournaments planned for Mondays and Tuesdays. Free card club rewards play with merchandise or restaurant and lodging comps. Generous comping policy for high-rollers. Some form of promotion—from free dinners to special tokens—occurs nearly every day. Coupon "fun books" are given to visitors who have traveled long distances.

Amenities: Lucky's Cafe offers a buffet on weekends or a standard menu featuring steaks, prime rib, or walleye in the evening, sandwiches during the day and breakfast anytime. Portions are generous and full-meal prices stay under $10. Local favorite: Country fried steak. Two bars, including a lounge and stage bar. Live music daily except Mondays. Liquor served in gaming areas. Video arcade near the hotel lobby. Gift shop.

Overnight: If you can't get into the 4 Bears lodge, the alternatives are bare-bones motels that casino employees describe as "clean and comfortable." Rates for the lodge are $55 on Fridays and Saturdays and $45 other nights, plus $5 each for the third or fourth person in the room. The casino also operates a nearby camping and RV park, complete with laundry and shower facilities and a 24-hour convenience store. Other lodging (all in New Town): West Dakota Inn, $32 for two, kitchenettes available (701-627-3721); Sunset Inn, $23–$37 (701-627-3316); Cottage Inn, kitchenettes available (701-627-4217).

Other Reasons to Be Here: Sailing and fishing are major summer activities. Uphill snowmobiling and hunting dominate the brisker months. Nearby is one of North Dakota's major wildlife management areas. The Crow Flies High Historic Site is a few miles north of New Town. To the west is the Little Missouri National Grassland and the north unit of Theodore Roosevelt National Park.

Prairie Knights Casino

Cannon Ball, North Dakota
800-425-8277

Getting There: 44 miles south of Mandan on Highway 1806. Take Interstate 94 west from Bismarck for seven miles, make a left exit into Mandan and turn left on Highway 1806. The road to the casino follows the west bank of the Missouri River's Oahe Reservoir.

First Impression: One of the best in the Midwest, though it gives new meaning to the expression "in the middle of nowhere."

Overview: When it opened in December of 1993, the $14 million Prairie Knights Casino attracted crowds who just wanted to see it, though many stayed to gamble.

More than $300,000 was spent on murals alone. Outside the main entrance, Arizona sculptor Snell Johnson created a huge bronze tableaux showing Native American hunters and their horses on the prairie. The casino's location is dramatic: high on a treeless hill between barren river bluffs and the man-made Oahe Reservoir. But the site poses transportation problems, even in a region where driving long distances is accepted as a way of life. Those traveling from the east can only cross the reservoir via bridges at Bismarck, some 50 miles north, or at Mobridge, S.D., nearly 100 miles south. Highway 1806, however, is a scenic route through a historic region.

The Casino: By any Midwestern standard, Prairie Knights is a fabulous place. The gaming area is a spacious circular room within a square-shaped building. Accents include fieldstone columns and a sheltered patio around the entire building that must be welcoming on blistering summer days. A circular ceiling mural high above the gaming area depicts traditional Native American prairie life. Enormous floor-to-ceiling murals also can be found in the buffet and restaurant. Both eating areas are showplaces; bargain prices don't exist here, but the quality of the food—and the way it is displayed—justify the expense. The Hunter's Club, with its elk-antler chandeliers, is embracingly quiet. And, we must repeat, there's no tipping allowed.

Not surprisingly, the gaming area is not a haven for bargain players, though nickel slot machines are available. There's only one $3-minimum blackjack table, though the $50 upper limit still keeps things fairly modest. During its first month of operation, a payout survey of casino slot machines by the gaming division of the North Dakota Attorney General's office placed Prairie Knights first in the state, with an average return of 93.1 percent.

Hours: 24 daily.

In Play: 400 slot and video games (video poker, keno), nickel to one-coin $5 machines; 12 blackjack tables ($3–$50) using six-deck shoes (four splits allowed; no double-downs after splits; splitting aces requires one additional card); one craps table ($50 limit) using standard Las Vegas layout; three poker tables ($50 maximum pot), offering stud and Texas Hold 'Em.

Specials: Progressives include a $1 "Break the Bank" slot jackpot that starts at $100,000. The North Dakota state blackjack tournament is held here in May. Various poker, blackjack and slot tournaments are offered during the year. Free "Club 7" card club rewards play with cash bonuses. Generous drink and dinner comping policy for high-rollers.

Amenities: The Feast of the Rock Buffet is open virtually around the clock, with the exception of an hour's prep time before lunch, supper and the midnight-to-dawn buffet. The Hunter's Club restaurant features upscale dining, including five-pound fresh Maine lobsters, an enormous 48-ounce porterhouse steak and a wine list with some three-figure prices. Two full bars have "appetizer" menus with finger-food and burger offerings, plus high-calorie desserts. Prices for drinks and food tend to be higher, but the casino has a strict no-tipping policy. The sunken show bar features live music nightly except Mondays. A teenager's arcade is adequate for short periods. The gift shop focuses almost exclusively on unusual Native American art and crafts.

Overnight: Prairie Knights is expected to become the centerpiece of a resort complex, though target dates for building depend on the success of the casino's first full year of operation. For now, visitors have to return to Mandan or Bismarck for lodging. Several chain hotels in Bismarck, including the Holiday Inn (701-255-6000) and the Radisson (701-258-7700), offer casino discounts.

Shuttle services: Harlow's, 701-224-1767; Luxury Tours, 701-258-5955; and Top Hat Limo, 701-223-9012.

Other Reasons to Be Here: The road from Mandan to the casino passes Fort Abraham Lincoln State Park, former home of the Seventh Cavalry under George Armstrong Custer. The 977-acre park focuses on historic military buildings, including the last home Custer built for his family, plus the On-A-Slant Indian village occupied by the Mandan Indians between 1650 and 1750. South of the casino, in the island community of Fort Yates, is Sitting Bull's burial site.

Daily cruises are available on the Missouri River aboard the *Lewis & Clark* riverboat from Memorial Day through Labor Day. Prices: $6.95–$10.95; Sunday family cruises, $22.95 for two adults and all dependents. Leaving from Bismarck, reservations required: 701-255-4233.

In winter, the Huff Hills Ski Resort, located on Highway 1806 north of the casino, is open from 10 A.M. to 5 P.M. Thursdays through Sundays. Lift rates are $12 and $8 on weekdays, $15 and $10 on weekends. Equipment is available for rent (701-663-6421).

Turtle Mountain Chippewa Casino

Belcourt, North Dakota
800-477-3497
701-477-3171 (Bingo)

Getting There: Five miles west of Belcourt on Highway 5. The casino is on a hill overlooking the highway.

First Impression: Certainly not flashy, but it's not just a joint.

Overview: Belcourt is a rustic community near the Canadian border in northeast North Dakota. There's nothing fancy about the town. Fishing on nearby Lake Metigoshe is a principal attraction, along with easy downhill skiing and snowmobiling in winter. Nearest city: Minot, N.D., about 110 miles southwest.

The Casino: Well, it's not a palace, but there's something very comfortable about it. This is the only casino in North Dakota that offers Indian dice, a game that utilizes a simple, rough-lumber version of a craps table and three dice. Players bet against each other and the casino takes a rake of each pot. Throwing a 1, 2, 3 is a craps, while any pair and a 6 is a natural, along with three of a kind or 4, 5 and 6. All other combinations yield a pair and a "point," which must be beaten by the next shooter. The casino itself is a long, low room, broken up with walls to allow for the Indian dice area, a small cafe and an additional back room slot facility. Unfortunately, the adjacent bingo hall is inadequately ventilated; you don't need to buy cigarettes to smoke there. Some expansion and upgrades are planned, but no major casino construction is anticipated.

Hours: 24 daily.

In Play: 300 slots and video games (video poker, keno), nickel to $1, including quarter progressives; eight blackjack tables ($2-$50), using six-deck shoes (dealer hits on soft 17s); three Indian dice tables ($25 maximum, three-person team required); three poker tables ($1 to $50 overall) offering stud and Texas Hold 'Em; 400-seat bingo hall featuring evening and some late-night sessions, plus Sunday matinees.

Specials: Indian dice tournaments on Thursdays and Sundays. Tuesday blackjack tournaments. Coupons available for some local motels and lodges. Special "fun book" for people who travel more than 50 miles to the casino.

Amenities: Full bar and adjacent restaurant that specializes in home cooking. The bingo hall also has a small snack bar.

Overnight: If you're looking for a resort experience, the locals recommend the Turtle Mountain Lodge, located about 10 miles north of Bottineau on Lake Metigoshe (701-263-4206). The resort features downhill and cross-country skiing in winter, fishing and other water recreation in summer. Full-service restaurant, coffee shop and pool. Rates: $34 single to $90 for an apartment suite that sleeps six. Other lodging: the Sleepy Teepee (701-477-3551), three miles east of the casino on Highway 5 in Belcourt, $35. A next-door restaurant provides room service and the casino offers coupons good for room discounts.

Note: The Turtle Mountain Band of Chippewa also operate a small "mini" casino on Highway 5 in Belcourt, which is part of a tribe-operated bowling alley and lounge. Aptly named, the mini is a grungy little room with 67 reel slot machines and two blackjack tables ($1–25 days, $2–$50 evenings). Unless it's convenient or you like grime, don't even bother.

CHAPTER 6

SOUTH DAKOTA

The Rules of the Game: You won't find any big casinos in South Dakota, but you'll find plenty of little ones—some of them pretty fancy. The Sunshine State also has its own alternative to Las Vegas: a little mining town out in the Black Hills called Deadwood, where the revenue from some 60 casinos has been used to preserve the memory of Wild Bill Hickok and Calamity Jane.

South Dakota permits reel-type slot machines, video games, blackjack and various forms of poker. The state also has a single bet limit of $5, which is supposed to keep all the games friendly.

With blackjack, for example, you can bet $5, split your hand for an additional $5 and double down on both hands for an additional $10. With poker, most casinos allow three rounds of $5 raises.

The only exception to the $5 wager limit is enjoyed by the Dakota Sioux Casino in Watertown, which negotiated a separate compact with the state that allows $100 betting limits on blackjack. A proposal to raise betting limits statewide was rejected by South Dakota voters in 1993.

Casino-style gambling in South Dakota exists in three forms:

• The video lottery. South Dakota law allows businesses that serve food and liquor to have up to 10 video lottery machines, with 36 percent of the gross revenue going to the state. Most of these machines are multi-game units that offer video poker, keno and slot-type games. In 1994, South Dakota's Supreme Court dropped a bombshell by ruling the state video lottery unconstitutional. The ruling endangered huge video-parlor centers that have grown up in placed like North Sioux City, where there are more than 100 parlors. State legislators scrambled to make South Dakota's video lottery comply with the state's constitution.

• Indian gaming. Five of South Dakota's nine tribes were running full-scale casinos in 1994 and three other tribes are expected to open casinos by the end of 1995. The ninth tribe, the Standing Rock Sioux, already operate a big casino in North Dakota near Bismarck.

• Deadwood casinos. In 1989, South Dakota lawmakers opened the door to casino gambling in Deadwood as a way of halting the rapid decay of this historic Old West mining town. Scores of small gaming houses now line historic Main Street, many in wonderfully restored old buildings.

South Dakota also limits the number of gambling devices (slot machines, blackjack and poker tables) in each casino. Indian casinos can have no more than 250 devices and each casino building in Deadwood can have no more than 30 devices.

You don't find many video poker machines in these casinos. The state's lottery system makes it possible to play video poker in virtually any corner bar, so most people go to casinos to play the reel-type slots or the table games. Some of the casinos install state video lottery machines to fill up their floor space, since the state machines don't count toward the maximum number of devices allowed under the casino law.

The Name of the Game: Gambling in South Dakota is highly seasonal, though most casinos manage to keep going with the local trade during the long, windy winters. As might be expected, the state's first-generation casinos are near major highways.

The Dakota Sioux Casino in Watertown and Royal River Casino in Flandreau are near Interstate 29, not far from the state's eastern border. The Lode Star and Golden Buffalo casinos require short drives north of Interstate 90 near Chamberlain in the center of the state. Deadwood is at the northern gateway to the Black Hills.

Three new Indian casinos were expected to open in South Dakota in 1994 or 1995. The Oglala Sioux had plans to build a casino near Hot Springs, at the southern gateway to the Black Hills. The Rosebud Sioux broke ground in 1994 on a casino just across the South Dakota border from Valentine, Neb. The third new casino will be on the Cheyenne River Reservation in the central part of the state.

Dakota Sioux Casino

Watertown, South Dakota
800-658-4717
605-882-2051

Getting There: 8 miles north of Watertown. Take Interstate 29 to the Waverly exit, then drive five miles west on Sioux Valley Road to the casino.

First Impression: A prairie hall.

South Dakota

50 Mi.

N

Watertown ①

② Deadwood

BLACK HILLS NATIONAL FOREST

Rapid City

90

Pierre

Fort Thompson

LOWER BRULE INDIAN RES.

④ ⑤ CROW CREEK INDIAN RES.

Flandreau ⑥

Lower Brule

83

Missouri R.

③ Lake Andes

Sioux Falls

29

Available games

S, B, P	①	**Dakota Sioux Casino:** Watertown
S, B, P	②	**Deadwood**
S, B, P	③	**Fort Randall Casino:** Lake Andes
S, B, P	④	**Golden Buffalo Casino:** Lower Brule
S, B, P	⑤	**Lode Star Casino:** Fort Thompson
S, B, P	⑥	**Royal River Casino:** Flandreau

S-Slot machines, **B**-Blackjack, **P**-Poker

Overview: Watertown (pop.: 17,500) is a prairie community not far from the state's eastern border. The casino is in the middle of a vast, flat-horizon land, shaded only by a new tribal water tower. One of the first Indian casinos in South Dakota, it is exempt from the state's $5 betting limit; blackjack bets can go as high as $100. Poker also is a major game here.

The Casino: The casino is a two-story, blue metal building, surrounded by a monstrous paved parking lot. Inside, however, it has been decked out like a western saloon, with red flocked wallpaper, antique-like light fixtures and lots of red velvet draperies. Miss Kitty would be comfortable here. A stairwell in the center leads to a large poker parlor and to a small deli that serves grill foods. The first level is divided into small playing areas, including two blackjack rooms and slot machine areas. The casino has a small restaurant, the Red Rose, that offers a buffet on weekends and specials every day. The Red Velvet Lounge is a cozy, diamond-shaped room, with good sight lines to a raised stage above the bar. The bar would be an agreeable place to hang out—and it's obvious that lots of people do exactly that.

Hours: 24 daily.

In Play: 250 slot machines, including a few video poker games, nickel to $1; 20 blackjack tables ($2–$100), using four-deck shoes (dealer hits on soft 17s, three splits allowed, splitting aces requires one additional card; no double-downs after splits); five poker tables ($1–$5 bets limited to three rounds), offering seven-card stud, Texas Hold 'Em and Omaha (rake: 10 percent to $3). Bingo hall in Sisseton, 50 miles north (605-698-7828).

Specials: Daily poker tournaments, with the house contributing to the cash pot. Double jackpots on slots are a regular feature. Call 800-658-4717 for information about blackjack tournaments and specials.

Amenities: The Red Velvet Lounge features live music for dancing every night and headliner stage shows every month. Sundays are senior days, with 50 percent discounts on the buffet. Prime Rib is featured on Tuesdays and Thursdays. Fun books distributed at hospitality desk. Liquor served in gaming area. Gift shop. Shuttle services to Watertown hotels.

Overnight: The Guest House Motor Inn in Watertown (800-356-7979) offers a $26 casino rate and amenities that include a restaurant, inside pool and a lounge. Watertown's 10 motels include the full-service Best Western Ramkota Inn (605-886-8011) and the Drake Motor Inn (800-252-4532). Other accommodations: Super 8 (605-882-1900), Traveler's Inn (605-882-2243) and the Elco Motel (800-769-ELCO).

Other Reasons to Be Here: Though a prairie community, Watertown has two major lakes: large and deep Lake Kampeska and shallow Lake Pelican. There are plenty of public campgrounds and parks. The Bramble Park Zoo is a pleasant little place. Recommended restaurant: The Office Bar and Restaurant, specializing in prime rib, steaks and seafood (605-886-2996).

Deadwood Casinos

Getting There: 40 miles northwest of Rapid City. Take Interstate 90 to Sturgis, then take Highway 14A to Deadwood.

Overview: The entire city is a National Historic Landmark, and a majority of its historic buildings have been turned into casinos. Once a gold-rush boom town, the little community of 2,000 is now booming in a different way on revenue from gambling that powers civic projects ranging from building renovations to new water and sewer systems. With varying success, the gaming halls reflect the Old West heritage of the community.

Deadwood capitalizes on a sordid history that began when George Armstrong Custer discovered gold in the Black Hills in 1874. Within a few years, the town located in a "gulch surrounded by dead wood" was filled with prospectors, prostitutes, gamblers and gunmen. Many attained lasting fame on the basis on their colorful names and reckless lifestyles—people like Wild Bill Hickok, Calamity Jane, Poker Alice, Preacher Smith, Potato Creek Johnny, and Deadwood Dick.

Deadwood's wild and woolly days were short-lived, however. Prospectors were soon replaced by mining-company employees. Tents and log cabins gave way to the civic and business buildings that are the landmarks of today.

In 1989, casino gambling was reintroduced in Deadwood as a way of raising money to restore the rapidly decaying Old West community. The city collects fees on each of the more than 2,500 gambling devices in Deadwood, takes a percentage of a general entertainment tax, and licenses the use of some 50 city-owned nickel slot machines.

Millions of people now visit Deadwood each year to gamble and take in the tourist attractions. Historic Main Street has been turned into an entertainment boulevard, lined with small casinos, restaurants and a few historic hotels. In summer, the community is awash with tourists, many of them senior citizens. Most visitors park on the edge of town and travel on a very efficient shuttle bus system (those who don't pay sky-high parking rates). Nearest city: Rapid City, 40 miles.

The Casinos: Officially, Deadwood has authority to issue 80 casino licenses. In order to avoid the construction of huge Las Vegas–style resort complexes, the licenses strictly limit the definition of a casino to 30 gambling devices (slot machines, blackjack or poker tables) in a single building.

A casino operator can hold as many as three casino licenses in three different buildings. In order to meet the requirements, many of Deadwood's larger casinos consist of three connected rooms—or "buildings"—each with a door to the street. Some of these three-building casinos place a different name over each entry door.

South Dakota's $5 bet limit prevails, though tales of big-buck poker sessions are common. Many of the casinos serve free beer to slot players. The larger casinos have buffets, restaurants and bars. Many of the smaller places are slot joints, with machines and a snack bar. A few exploit themes: At B.B. Cody's, for example, bar patrons sit on saddles instead of stools and drink under a mural that features stuffed buffalo heads emerging from a painted prairie scene.

The younger party crowd tends to patronize Old Style Saloon No. 10, which has sawdust on the rough-lumber floor and a stage for rock bands in the corner. The saloon takes its name from the place where Wild Bill Hickok was gunned down in 1876 while playing poker. The upscale Midnight Star, owned by actor Kevin Costner, attracts a young, better-dressed crowd to its lavish bar and entertainment complex. Costner's movie costumes are on display in glass cases and posters from his films are everywhere.

The mini-Vegas feel, by contrast, can be experienced at the Silverado or the Gold Dust Entertainment Complex. Both are big operations by Deadwood standards. The Gold Dust is a popular stop for first-time visitors, who join its slot club and collect the club's easy-to-get first premium: a free meal.

At the other end of town are a few wholly new casinos, among them Tin Lizzie's, which boasts free parking, and Four Aces, which has a big restaurant and about 90 gambling devices. Most of the city's motels and hotels also have gambling halls.

A sampling of the casinos:

Bazel's Gaming Hall, 668 Main St. $1 afternoon blackjack; two-deck pitch games.

Bella Union, 645 Main St. Arcade for children, single-deck blackjack.

Bodega Bar & Cafe, 662 Main St. One of Deadwood's oldest saloons, beautifully restored. Restaurant has children's menu.

Bullock Hotel, 633 Main St. Live entertainment, children's arcade in the basement.

Butch Cassidy Saloon, 59 Sherman St. Casino has a separate arcade room for kids.

Dakota Territory Saloon, 652 Main St. A haven for poker players, featuring a $2,000 Hold 'Em good-beat jackpot.

Days Inn Casino, 68 Main St. The hotel's small casino is augmented by a special gaming package with Miss Kitty's Saloon on Main Street.

Deadwood Dick's Saloon, 55 Sherman St. Big arcade for the kids and a big selection of Deadwood Dick shirts and caps.

Deadwood Gulch Resort, South Highway 85. The biggest jackpot in Deadwood—$743,000—was won here on a Quartermania slot machine.

Eagle Bar, 622 Main St. Live music on weekends.

Fairmont Hotel/Oyster Bay, 622 Main St. Specializes in seafood; oyster bar in summer.

First Gold Hotel & Gaming Complex, 270 Main St. 24-hour casino, plus children's movie arcade.

Four Aces, 531 Main St. Upscale surroundings; large dining area; complimentary buffet for poker players.

Historic Franklin Hotel, 700 Main St. Two Irish pubs and a 1903 dining room. Deadwood's largest historic hotel, still being restored.

Gold Dust Entertainment Complex, 688 Main St. Part of a complex that includes the Gold Dust, Silver Dollar and French Quarter casinos.

Gold Nugget Casino, 801 Main St. Large collection of antique slot machines.

Goldbergs Gaming, 672 Main St. A 24-hour complex that includes Big Jake's Card Room and Sophie's Slots and Sodas, with its long marble fountain counter.

Golddiggers, 629 Main St. A 24-hour place with a "Big Bertha" $1 slot machine.

Jackpot Charlie's and the Green Door Club, 616 Main St. Beautifully restored tin ceiling and gorgeous flocked wallpaper.

Lady Luck, 660 Main St. Breakfast specials include homemade sausage, eggs and hash browns for $1.99.

Lucky Miner, 651 Main St. Quarter beer and free entertainment for children.

Lucky Wrangler, 638 Main St. Italian food, movies and refreshments for children.

Midnight Star, 677 Main St. Kevin Costner's four-story glamour palace, featuring a top-rated restaurant, plus a very trendy card room.

Mineral Palace, 601 Main St. Treasure Linked Jackpot slot machine starts at $100,000.

Miss Kitty's, 649 Main St. The best Chinese restaurant in Deadwood.

Motherlode Gaming Saloon, 155 Sherman St. Huge dance floor for country and country-rock entertainers.

Old Style Saloon No. 10, 657 Main St. Sawdust on the floor and "artifacts" from the 1876 shooting of Wild Bill Hickok. Bands play nightly during the summer. Deadwood's best-known watering hole.

Shedd Jewelers Gold En Gaming, 674 Main St. America's only jewelry store with a casino and pub.

Silverado, 709 Main St. Big casino features Cadillac jackpots.

Overnight: Rates vary widely according to the season. Moderately appointed rooms tend to be priced high in the summer and dirt cheap in the winter. It's best to call ahead for reservations during the summer season. And, of course, it's impossible to find a place to stay during the Sturgis motorcycle rally in early August.

Some choices:

Adams House Bed & Breakfast, 22 Van Buren St. (605-578-3877). A Queen Anne home built in 1892 features original wallpaper and furniture. Four rooms. No children under 12. $65–$90.

All Season's Budget Motel, Highway 85 and 385 (605-578-2529). Kitchenettes available. 18 rooms. $25–$80.

Best Western Hickok House, 137 Charles St. (800-528-1234). Casino, arcade, sauna, whirlpool and restaurant on premises. 38 rooms. $35–$89.

Bullock Hotel, 633 Main St. (800-336-1876). A lavish restoration of a major Main Street hotel, complete with antique replicas and Jacuzzi suites. 28 rooms. $25–$115.

Cedar Wood Inn, 103 Charles St. (800-841-0127). Playground; refrigerators and coffeepots in rooms. 18 rooms. $25–$75.

Days Inn '76 Motel, 68 Main St. (800-526-8277). Casino, restaurant on premises. 38 rooms. $56–$75.

Deadwood Gulch Resort, South Highway 85 (800-695-1876). Restaurant, casino, bar, heated outdoor pool, arcade. 97 rooms. $35–$85.

First Gold Hotel and 4-U Motel, 270 Main St. (800-274-1876) Casino, restaurant and lounge. RV hookups. $32–$79.

Golddiggers Hotel, 629 Main St. (800-456-2023). Deluxe service for casino guests, including complimentary champagne and breakfast. Nine rooms. $79–$129.

Gold Nugget Inn, 801 W. Main St. (605-578-2393). Cafe and slot room. 53 rooms. $40–$75.

Franklin Hotel, 700 Main St. (800-688-1876). Large historic hotel in the heart of the gaming district, now being restored. 75 Rooms. $48–$150.

Jackpot Inn, Highway 835 South (800-756-6337). Outdoor hot tub. 45 rooms. $20–$64.

Lariat Motel, 360 Main St. (800-773-1503). Suites available. 20 rooms. $40–$90.

Mineral Palace, 601 Main St. (605-578-2036). Lavish suite with wet bar and fireplace. All-new hotel with historic facade. 63 rooms. $59–$159.

Penny Motel, 818 Main St. (605-578-1842). Breakfast coupons available, pets allowed. 14 rooms. $30–$48.

Super 8 Lodge, 196 Cliff St. (800-800-8000). Complimentary breakfast, indoor pool. 51 rooms. $49–$150.

Terrace Motel, 250 Main St. (800-851-5699). Senior citizen discounts. 27 rooms. $30–$60.

Vicky's Bed and Breakfast, 786 Main St. (800-606-2279). Breakfast served at Sassy's fine restaurant. Two rooms. Rates vary.

Other Reasons to Be Here: Start your visit at the Adams Museum, 54 Sherman St., which provides a historical overview of Deadwood. Items on display include Potato Creek Johnny's gold nugget, weapons carried by the city's rough founders, and the first locomotive in the Black Hills. Open daily, donations requested.

The Alkali Ike Bus Tour (605-578-3147) is a one-hour ride that includes a visit to Mt. Moriah, the famous Boot Hill cemetery. A similar tour, this one endorsed by the Lawrence County Historical Society, departs daily at 11 A.M. 1, 3 and 5:30 P.M. from the Bodega Cafe on Main Street. $5 adults, $2.50 children. You can also walk to Mt. Moriah Cemetery, pay $1 (50 cents for children), and climb the steep hills to view the cemetery's many famous residents—Wild Bill Hickok and Calamity Jane among them—from a maintained path.

The Broken Boot Gold Mine on Highway 14A at the outskirts of Deadwood offers a 20-minute underground tour of a gold mine as it looked in the late 1800s. Group rates are available (605-578-1876).

The Ghosts of Deadwood Gulch Wax Museum, 12 Lee St., features Indian leaders, explorers, soldiers and the city's legendary gold-rush characters. Open May through September (605-578-3585).

The House of Roses Museum, 15 Forest Ave., overlooks historic Main

Street and features 27 rooms of antiques. Open all year, 9 A.M. to 6 P.M., or by appointment (605-578-1879).

"The Trial of Jack McCall" reenacts the events that took place on Aug. 2, 1876, when McCall shot Wild Bill Hickok during a poker game. During the summer, the assassin is captured on Main Street every night except Sundays and brought to trial in the theater at 12 Lee St., site of the wax museum. You can reserve seats at the museum or call 605-578-3583.

Fort Randall Casino & Hotel

Lake Andes, South Dakota
800-553-3003
605-487-7871

Getting There: From Interstate 90, take Exit 310 at Highway 281 and drive about 60 miles south and west, following signs to the casino on Highway 46. From Interstate 29, follow Highway 46 or Highway 50 west, about 70 miles, then follow signs at Pickstown.

First Impression: One sign is not enough.

Overview: South Dakota's southeastern border is a major farming and recreational area. The Ft. Randall Dam, just west of Pickstown, created a huge long lake that is a summer haven for fishing, swimming and sailing. Farther downstream, the dam at Yankton created the narrow, tree-lined Lewis & Clark Reservoir. In fall, the area near Wagner is renowned for pheasant hunting. Built in 1856, Fort Randall was one of the first military outposts on the upper Missouri River, and it operated until 1892. The remains of the fort's chapel are a popular historic site. Nearest city: Yankton, 50 miles east.

The Casino: From the outside, it looks like the builders of the Fort Randall Casino took their inspiration from South Dakota's famous Wall Drug Store. The long, wood-sided building is festooned with signs, advertising the hotel, saloon, bingo and gambling halls, and the various games available inside. The casino, which sits atop a treeless hill, emulates the rough-sawn appearance of an Old West town, offering a facade of false-peaked roofs. Inside, however, it's more like a conventional hotel and conference center. The casino is a complex of low-ceiling rooms, feeling very claustrophobic. An effort has been made to create gambling venues: blackjack in a sunken area, poker in a cramped, walled-off room, slots in nooks and crannies. The complex has a large dining area, a big bingo hall and a lounge with a full-sized, curtained stage. In all, it's a big place that still manages to feel cramped.

Hours: 24 daily.

In Play: 240 slot machines, nickel to $1. 14 blackjack tables ($2–$5), using four-deck shoes (no double downs after splits; splitting aces requires one additional card). Three poker tables offering seven-card stud, Omaha, and Texas Hold 'Em ($5 limits on raises over three rounds; house rake of 10 percent to $3 per pot). Caribbean stud planned as part of expansion. 300-seat bingo hall has nightly sessions except Tuesdays, plus matinees on weekends.

Specials: Blackjack tournaments on Mondays. Poker tournaments announced as promotions. Many bingo specials.

Amenities: Lounge offers afternoon and evening entertainment daily, plus frequent headliner stage shows. Large bar, plus liquor served in gaming areas. "Big plate" buffet all day, plus menu items. Sandwich deli.

Overnight: Attached hotel has 57 rooms and two suites, $25–$45, (800-553-3003).

Other Reasons to Be Here: The Fort Randall Dam and Recreation Area provides swimming, boating, sailing and other outdoor activities. The Randall Hills Golf Course is a statewide attraction. Historic sites include ruins of the fort built in 1856. Boaters often visit the Lewis & Clark Resort & Marina in Yankton, about 50 miles east of the casino, which has cabins (605-665-4186).

Golden Buffalo Casino

Lower Brule, South Dakota
800-658-4554
605-473-5577

Getting There: Take the Reliance exit (No. 248) from Interstate 90 and go north on Highway 47 for eight miles, then seven miles west on a BIA road to Lower Brule.

First Impression: The end of the trail, pard.

Overview: You cross a treeless prairie, filled with amber waves of grain and grazing cattle, as you drive to Lower Brule, a small Indian community on the banks of a section of the Missouri River that is known to fishermen as Lake Sharp. It's a dusty, bustling town, with two schools, a new bank and resort businesses relating to the casino, which opened in 1992. Before the casino, most visitors to Lower Brule came for the walleyes and to hunt buffalo and elk at a nearby big-game park. Today, the casino is the anchor for a modest hotel and restaurant, plus a nearby camping and RV park. Nearest city: Pierre, about 30 miles northwest.

The Casino: The casino is a boxy, two-story building with an attached one-story restaurant that can be entered without walking through the gaming area. Across a parking lot is a 38-room hotel that was erected in 1994. Inside, the casino is a pleasant, Perkins restaurant–like place, with a high ceiling, bright lights and a bar extending along one side of the gaming hall. The walls are decorated with Indian and Western art. Hidden from view is a small, 125-seat bingo hall that also doubles as a buffet and entertainment room on weekends. The Golden Buffalo was one of the first casinos in South Dakota to introduce multi-action blackjack, where players can bet against three hands by the dealer. It remains a popular game because of the state's $5 bet limit. The casino is only 13 miles from the Lode Star Casino at Fort Thompson, which opened in 1993. Regular customers tend to patronize both establishments.

Hours: 9 A.M. to 1 A.M. Mondays through Thursdays; 24 hours Fridays through Sundays.

In Play: 120 slot machines and four video poker machines, mostly nickel to $1, with several $5 machines. 12 blackjack tables ($2–$5), using six-deck shoes (four splits allowed with double-downs permitted except for split aces, which require one additional card; $4 bets required to play two hands; $5 to play three or more hands). Three poker tables for seven-card stud, Texas Hold 'Em and high-low ($5 maximum raises for three rounds; house rake of 10 percent to $3 per pot).

Specials: Slot tournaments planned. Blackjack tournaments scheduled during promotions. Call casino for information on bingo sessions.

Amenities: Liquor served in gaming area ($1.25 beer, $2.25 bar brand drinks). Restaurant serves a $4.95 prime rib dinner every day. Buffets on Wednesday and Saturday nights in the bingo hall, plus Sundays at noon. Live music on Saturday nights.

Overnight: 38-room hotel, located across the parking lot from the casino, features an indoor pool, sauna, video game room and gift shop. Room rates are less than $50 (800-658-4554).

Other Reasons to Be Here: The ZiZi Tatanka Stampede Rodeo is held here in July, attracting thousands of visitors. The Lower Brule Pow Wow takes place the second week of August. The tribe also operates a 60-site RV and camping park on the Missouri River, about four blocks from the casino. Call 800-658-4554 for information.

Lode Star Casino

Fort Thompson, South Dakota
605-245-6000

Getting There: 23 miles north of Chamberlain on Highway 50. Take Exit 263 from Interstate 90 and drive north.

First Impression: Desert Storm vets will be right at home.

Overview: Casinos are not plentiful in South Dakota, yet the Lode Star Casino and the Golden Buffalo Casino are less than 13 miles apart, separated by different Indian reservations on each side of the Missouri River and connected by the road across Big Bend Dam. But most patrons drive to the competing casinos from I-90, taking winding roads through the scenic foothills of the Missouri River. Highway 50 to the Lode Star provides a series of panoramic river vistas, but the road is narrow and treacherous at night. Once you reach Fort Thompson, you discover a once-neglected Indian community that is now in the process of rehabilitating its housing and streets. Improvements include a new housing development and a center for the community's senior citizens. Nearest city: Pierre, about 60 miles northwest.

The Casino: In 1993, the Crow Creek tribe used building technology tested in Operation Desert Storm to erect a temporary casino out of space-age plastic over a steel frame. The results look like a big greenhouse in a sandwich bag. Inside, however, this small casino is astonishingly complete, though in miniature. There are no enclosed rooms. Instead, each area—such as the poker room, the restaurant and the lounge—has been defined by a short wall or sometimes a false arch. The casino is very small, but it seems a lot bigger. Pleasing colors and a black-painted plastic ceiling add to the effect. Nonetheless, the plastic casino is not without its problems, especially when the temperatures outside are sub-zero, or when tornado season visits the prairie.

Casino officials say the temporary casino will be replaced by a large casino resort complex closer to the Missouri—one that will include a theater, hotel, marina, golf course and other amenities.

Hours: 24 daily during warmer months. 10 A.M. to 2 A.M. or 4 A.M. in winter.

In Play: 140 slot and video poker games, nickel to $1. Eight blackjack tables ($2–$5), using four-deck shoes (splitting aces requires one additional card). Three poker tables for seven-card stud and Texas Hold 'Em ($5 raise limit over three rounds, house rake 10 percent to $3 a pot). Nightly bingo sessions at the Fort Thompson Bingo Hall.

Specials: Blackjack tournaments Mondays and Tuesdays. Poker tournaments every weekend. "Silver Star" slot club returns cash for gambling activity and beeps irritatingly every time you earn a point on a slot machine.

Amenities: Dakota Prime restaurant offers a prime rib special on Saturdays. Full bar and small lounge, which has entertainment on weekends during warm weather. Extensive promotional programs include coupons for visitors who drove more than 50 miles, plus discounts on hotels in Chamberlain. Limo and shuttle service to Chamberlain.

Overnight: The Days Inn (605-734-4100) in Oacoma, just off I-90 at Exit 260, offers casino packages. The same exit takes you to Al's Oasis, the largest highway stop in South Dakota. The Oasis Inn ($35 single), part of the Al's Oasis complex, is run by the Kelly Inn organization and has its own hot tub and sauna, plus a free fishing pond (800-635-3559). In Chamberlain, try Lee's Best Western Motor Inn, which has an indoor pool, free movies and 10 two-room suites (800-528-1234).

Other Reasons to Be Here: The large lake created at Chamberlain, plus its shallow backwaters, is famous for fishing (South Dakota's season never closes) and hunting. The Akta Lakota Museum in Chamberlain, featuring Sioux art and artifacts, is open from May through September. Free admission. The Crow Creek and Lower Brule Indian communities host fairs and rodeos each summer, plus powwows the second and third weekends in August.

Royal River Casino & Bingo

Flandreau, South Dakota
800-234-2946

Getting There: Take Interstate 29 to Highway 32 exit. Go seven miles east to Flandreau. Signs make the casino easy to find.

First Impression: Home of South Dakota's largest serving plate, by golly.

Overview: Flandreau is a farming community seven miles from the Minnesota border. Royal River is the closest casino to Sioux Falls, which is about 40 miles south. The casino is part of a tribe-owned complex that includes a large bingo hall, planned entertainment pavilion, a convenience store/cafe and a motel. It gets its name from the nearby Big Sioux River.

The Casino: From the outside, Royal River looks like a Ponderosa Steak House, a long building with rough-sawn siding and cross-hatched entry doors. Inside, a series of expansions has taken a toll; the casino is not pleasingly designed, though it's comfortable. It's a pink neon place, with metal beams exposed in the low ceiling. Cheaply priced food and drink are major attractions—especially the buffet, with its highly advertised Hulk Hogan–size serving plates. The bar serves name-brand liquors at a steeply discounted price to gamblers, but adds a buck or more if you aren't playing. A new entertainment venue was planned for 1994 to replace the tiny upstairs balcony that is currently used for bands and small stage acts.

Hours: 24 daily.

In Play: 238 slot and video poker games, nickel to three-coin $1 machines. Nine blackjack tables ($2–$5), using six-deck shoes. Three poker tables, offering Texas Hold 'Em ($2–$5 limits) and seven-card stud ($1–$3 and $2–$5 limits). Quarter poker played daily between 9 A.M. and 4 P.M. For daily bingo schedule in the adjacent hall, call the casino's toll-free number.

Specials: Blackjack tournaments on some Mondays and Tuesdays. Frequent poker tournaments. Poker room has bad beat prize for the week.

Amenities: 24-hour buffet, plus full-service dining featuring prime rib and crab legs. Full bar, with snack food. Live music most weekends and occasional stage shows. Free shuttle service to Sioux Falls operates around the clock.

Overnight: The First American Inn, basically a small-town motel, is within sight of the casino and is operated by the tribe; call 800-234-2946 for reservation information. In Sioux Falls, dozens of motels offer more than 2,300 rooms; call the city's convention bureau (605-336-1620) to learn about lodging. Pipestone, a Minnesota community less than 20 miles from Flandreau, has the historic Calumet Inn, an elegant hotel built in the nineteenthth century (800-535-7610).

Other Reasons to Be Here: South Dakota's largest shopping mall is the Sioux Empire Mall in Sioux Falls. The Pipestone National Monument in nearby Pipestone, Minn., maintains the quarry used by Native Americans to produce ceremonial objects; the community's Hiawatha Pageant, performed near the monument, is a fixture of summer entertainment.

CHAPTER 7

WISCONSIN

The Rules of the Game: Casino gambling in Wisconsin belongs to its Native American nations. Other forms of gambling include four highly unprofitable dog-racing tracks, a state lottery, and charitable-gambling activities like bingo, raffles and pull-tabs. State law permits parimutuel betting on horses and snowmobile races, but no licenses have been granted for these activities. Some bars have slot-type games, but the legality of these machines is still being debated.

State authorities began signing gaming compacts with Native American tribes in 1991, though some tribes were already operating casinos in 1988, when the federal Indian Gaming Regulatory Act was passed. The compacts allow slot machines and video games, plus the standard form of casino blackjack—with a $200 maximum on opening bets.

In addition to tight requirements for video surveillance, computer-chip security and accounting, all non-skill slot machines must return between 80 and 100 percent in payouts. The requirement for "skill" games, such as video poker, is a payout of between 83 and 100 percent. Casinos are not required to post average slot paybacks, though some advertise that their machines return up to 94.7 percent. The compacts allow each tribe to operate two casinos in addition to bingo halls. Some tribes have stretched the definitions. The Winnebagos, for example, have three casinos—though the Majestic Pines facility near Black River Falls offers only bingo and slot machines; the tribe calls it a bingo hall when dealing with state officials. The Potawatomi tribe runs a gigantic bingo and slot house in Milwaukee, which is technically not a casino, according to the tribe.

In 1994, a consortium of three tribes announced plans to convert the St. Croix Meadows dog track near Hudson into a huge casino and track. However, the plan faces some stiff political and legal hurdles and state officials predict it may be years before such a facility opens—if at all.

The Name of the Game: Depending on how you count them, there are 14 to 22 casinos in Wisconsin. State gaming authorities lump Indian-operated bingo halls in the same listings with casinos, though the legal definitions are different. Generally, however, the casinos are evenly spread across the central and northern parts of the state. As might be expected, the casinos in the northern part of the state tend to be more rustic, while the upscale operations are near major highways, resort areas and large cities.

It's possible to lose big money at Wisconsin casinos, but the $200 cap on blackjack betting tends to set a more conservative tone to casino play. The state's biggest casino, the Oneida in Green Bay, has a high-stakes area, but it's hard to establish that big-player aura when high stakes means a bunch of $5 single-coin slot machines and tables where most people are betting $25 a pop.

Besides, most Wisconsin players aren't into glitz. Most of the casinos in the northern part of the state are homey, oversized roadhouses that cater to nickel and quarter slot players and do a big business with the charter-bus crowd. Competition from Minnesota casinos often centers on the types of slots—which are "real reel" in Wisconsin and, by law, must be video in Minnesota. It's all a question of taste, of course, since all modern slot machines are controlled by computer chips.

There are notable exceptions, but as a general rule, Wisconsin casinos don't put much emphasis on fine dining. Wisconsin is the land of the beer joint and steak house, and it may be that the casinos have been careful—and politically prudent—about trying to capture the food trade. For whatever reason, you're likely to encounter a snack bar or deli at most casinos. The liquor trade is another matter; at most Wisconsin casinos, the booze flows like water and usually dribbles into the gaming areas.

Bad River Casino

Odanah, Wisconsin
715-682-7131

Getting There: On Highway 2, 10 miles east of Ashland, Wis., and 10 miles west of Ironwood, Mich. The casino is right along the highway.

First Impression: This must be the best place to find lumberjacks.

Overview: The area around Bad River Casino would be a perfect location to make a TV car commercial, showing a sleek new vehicle cruising along a solitary highway that cuts through an impenetrable forest. While this seems like wilderness country, it's only a short distance to Ashland, with its Lake Superior resorts, and Ironwood, Mich.

The Casino: American and Canadian flags decorate the entry doors to this small, log-sided gambling den, which looks more like a lodge than a casino.

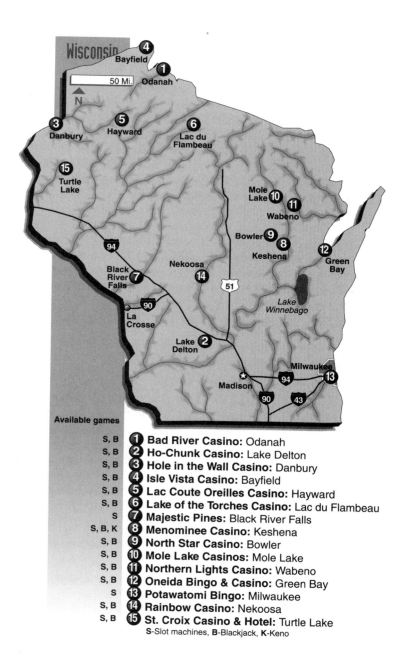

Wisconsin

Bayfield
50 Mi.
Odanah

N

Danbury

Hayward

Lac du
Flambeau

Turtle
Lake

Mole
Lake

Wabeno

Bowler

Keshena

Nekoosa

Green
Bay

Black
River
Falls

La
Crosse

Lake
Winnebago

Lake
Delton

Milwaukee

Madison

Available games

S, B	①	**Bad River Casino:** Odanah
S, B	②	**Ho-Chunk Casino:** Lake Delton
S, B	③	**Hole in the Wall Casino:** Danbury
S, B	④	**Isle Vista Casino:** Bayfield
S, B	⑤	**Lac Coute Oreilles Casino:** Hayward
S, B	⑥	**Lake of the Torches Casino:** Lac du Flambeau
S	⑦	**Majestic Pines:** Black River Falls
S, B, K	⑧	**Menominee Casino:** Keshena
S, B	⑨	**North Star Casino:** Bowler
S, B	⑩	**Mole Lake Casinos:** Mole Lake
S, B	⑪	**Northern Lights Casino:** Wabeno
S, B	⑫	**Oneida Bingo & Casino:** Green Bay
S	⑬	**Potawatomi Bingo:** Milwaukee
S, B	⑭	**Rainbow Casino:** Nekoosa
S, B	⑮	**St. Croix Casino & Hotel:** Turtle Lake

S-Slot machines, **B**-Blackjack, **K**-Keno

It's a narrow, two-story building with blackjack tables on the second floor, along with a nickel slot parlor, and quarter and dollar slots on the ground level. A little walk-up counter serves liquor, though this is beer country—and the beer comes in cans. Video poker appears to be the dominant game, and the machines, including the nickel versions and progressives, are among the best in Wisconsin, with a theoretical payout of about 97 percent. The whole interior is paneled in knotty pine and the best spot is in the back, where the original building features massive log beams and a huge stone fireplace with, alas, a gas log.

Expansion plans call for a small, 42-room hotel resort and a doubling in the size of the gaming area. The rustic decor will be maintained.

Hours: 10 A.M. to 2 A.M. daily.

In Play: 222 slot and video games (keno, poker, blackjack), nickel to $1 machines. Eight blackjack tables ($2–$200) using four-deck shoes (dealer hits on soft 17; double downs allowed after splits; splitting aces requires one additional card). Bingo played Wednesdays through Sundays in a building about a mile away.

Specials: Four progressive slots, quarter to $1.

Amenities: Liquor served in the gaming area, at $1.25 a drink. A recently expanded restaurant serves daily specials and a buffet.

Overnight: The casino provides shuttle services to hotels in Ironwood, Mich., and Ashland; call 715-682-7131 for information. In Ashland, the Hotel Chequamegon, $50–$110, stands on the shores of Lake Superior, like a huge white birthday cake (800-946-5555 or 715-682-9095). Its restaurant is recommended by locals. Anderson's Chequamegon Motel ($30–$56) is much smaller, but carries a two-star AAA rating and is adjacent to a Lake Superior beach and popular snowmobile trail (715-682-4658). Other lodging: Best Western Holiday House, $38–$75 (800-528-1234); Ashland Super 8, $38–$58 (800-800-8000).

Other Reasons to Be Here: You're in the outdoors, which means hunting, fishing, cross-country skiing, snowmobiling and the attractions of chilly Lake Superior.

Ho-Chunk Casino

Baraboo, Wisconsin
800-746-2486
608-356-6210

Getting There: Five miles south of Lake Delton on Highway 12. From I-94, take Exit 92, marked "Highway 12 East."

First Impression: Don't forget the water show and the famous "ducks."

Overview: It may be debated whether the Wisconsin Dells is an appropriate place for a casino, but the state's leading recreation area has one that's consistent with the Dells glitz—a $20 million mall with two restaurants, an entertainment venue and 1,200 slot machines. Detractors call this area of Wisconsin the Land of Vulgarity, dominated by mini-golf, go-kart tracks and water parks. It's got all that, plus the venerable Tommy Bartlett Water Show, featuring clowns and pretty girls on water skis, and the tours of the Dells in old World War II landing craft called "ducks." Some say the Dells region is a monument to the truly tasteless, but lots of people love this place. Nearest city: Madison, Wis., 53 miles.

The Casino: When it opened late in 1993, the Ho-Chunk became the second-largest employer in the Dells area, with nearly 1,000 employees and a $25 million annual payroll. The casino is a big pastel-and-neon hall surrounded by a blacktop parking lot that required enough bituminous paving—about 1,800 tons—to surface an 11-mile highway. Inside, the colors tend toward teal and magenta and the place has a big, airy feeling, though there's not a lot of fancy trim. Slot machines dominate, of course, and the reported payback on the mechanicals is 90.3 cents on the dollar. The buffet restaurant is good, though not outstanding, and there's a snack bar that offers fast food. The adjacent bingo hall is used for entertainment, mostly the country-and-western variety. The casino was designed to provide liquor beverage service, but the issue of allowing liquor on the premises is still being debated. Expansion plans include a possible facility for entertaining the kids.

Hours: 24 daily.

In Play: 1,200 slot and video games (video poker, keno), nickel to $1 machines; 48 blackjack tables ($3–$200), using six-deck shoes (splitting aces requires one additional card, with double-downs allowed after splits). Daily bingo sessions.

Specials: Blackjack tournaments on Tuesdays ($50 registration, $35 reentry). The casino's toll telephone number (608-356-6210) provides recorded information on upcoming events and tournaments.

Amenities: The buffet offers a $5.50 lunch and $8.75 dinner.

Overnight: The Dells may have the largest concentration of privately operated resorts and motels in Wisconsin. Rates vary radically according to the season. Top-rated places include Bakers Sunset Bay Resort, $38–$145, (608-254-8406), and Chula Vista Resort, $89–$300 (608-254-8366), but there's also everything from state and private campgrounds to mom-and-pop motels. Highly recommended: Christmas Mountain Village,

$59–$89 (608-254-3988), which has a complete menu of golf, skiing, and other amenities, plus a secluded setting.

Other Reasons to Be Here: The Dells. Don't worry, you'll find something.

Hole in the Wall Casino

Danbury, Wisconsin
800-238-8946
715-656-3444

Getting There: In Danbury at the intersection of Highways 35 and 77.

First Impression: A hole in name only.

Overview: Danbury is a small crossroads community that lies in the heart of a peaceful, backwoods region. Most people who come here own or rent cabins that surround the many shallow, interconnected lakes in the area. A major activity, in addition to fishing, is gazing at the woods across the lake as the sun sets (or rises). Few people thought the Hole in the Wall Casino would survive when the huge Grand Casino resort complex opened near Hinckley in Minnesota, just 27 miles away. But after three years, Danbury's casino has thrived by capitalizing on its small size, its pleasant, off-beat atmosphere and its "real reel" slot machines. Expansions have made Hole in the Wall a fairly nice-sized casino. A 38-room motel was added in 1992–93. In 1994, the casino added another section to its long, skinny building and put in an RV park and campground in a nearby wooded area next to the Yellow River. Nearest city: Duluth, Minn., 50 miles.

The Casino: A series of additions has turned a small, pine-sided structure into a long, one-story snake of a building that still retains that northwoods feel. Lumberjacks would play here—and probably do. Inside, the casino is a long, low-ceiling hall with slot machines and blackjack tables. Cocktails are served in the gaming area from a small service bar, though patrons here tend to make a big run on the free coffee. The Loose Change Cafe is an unpretentious, country coffee shop, with daily specials like tuna salad on toast. Once or twice a month, the casino hires one or two musicians, who find a spot somewhere, open their guitar cases and perform.

Hours: 8 A.M. to 2 A.M. weekdays, 8 A.M. to 4 A.M. Fridays and Saturdays.

In Play: 400 slot and video games (video poker, keno), nickel to $1. 12 blackjack tables ($2–$100), using six-deck shoes (four splits allowed, double downs allowed after splits, except for aces, which require one additional card). Bingo hall operates in a separate building; call 715-656-3227 for session times.

Amenities: Liquor (75-cent tap beer, $1.50 drinks) served in gaming area. Shuttle buses provided to the Duluth-Superior area. 80-seat café. Membership in the free Hole Card Club includes a plastic ID card with a hole in it.

Overnight: The Hole in the Wall Casino Hotel, $30–$50, has a few rooms, plus a small video arcade (715-656-4333). Other lodging in Danbury: Johnson's Motel (715-656-4050). A favorite resort motel in the area is the Forgotten Tymes in Siren, $80–$125 (715-349-5837).

Other Reasons to Be Here: Well, there's the woods, and you should bring your boat. Snowmobiling and cross-country skiing are popular in winter. Just across the state line is St. Croix State Park, the largest state park in Minnesota. Some of the many local taverns offer dancing and music.

Isle Vista Casino

Bayfield, Wisconsin
800-226-8478
715-779-3712

Getting There: Three miles north of Bayfield on Highway 13. The casino is on a small hill overlooking Lake Superior.

First Impression: Jeesh, this looks like a bowling alley. Yikes, it is!

Overview: Bayfield, known as the gateway to Lake Superior's Apostle Islands, is as north as you can get in Wisconsin. This picturesque, hilly village of 1,700 people is littered with tourist shops and resorts. In summer, yelling "Hey, sailor" will get everyone's attention, because this is yacht country. In winter, four-wheel drive is recommended. Nearest city: Duluth, Minn., 80 miles.

The Casino: This place has all the aura of a truck stop. The sign across the front of the low, flat-topped building says Red Cliff Lanes & Bingo Center. The casino is a recent addition to the "complex": a rectangular, one-room gambling den between the bowling alley and the bingo hall. One long wall of the room has been painted, floor-to-ceiling, with a folk-style mural depicting traditional Ojibwe life. There's a help-yourself pop and coffee counter in the back, plus a window to buy snacks. It's a clean, unpretentious, low-bet place with no real surprises. Approval has been given to construct a new casino and resort complex at a different location in Bayfield. Earliest completion date: 1995.

Hours: 10 A.M. to midnight Sunday–Tuesday; 10 A.M. to 2 A.M. Wednesday–Saturday.

In Play: 175 slot and video games (video poker, keno), nickel to $1 machines. Eight blackjack tables ($2–$200), using six-deck shoes (four splits allowed; no surrenders; splitting aces requires one additional card).

Specials: Occasional slot tournaments. Blackjack tournaments every Wednesday require a $5 entry fee, winner take all. A $1,000 blackjack tournament is usually held on the last Monday of the month, requiring a $15 entry fee.

Amenities: Bands provide music every Friday and Saturday in the big tavern/restaurant next to the bowling alley, where there's also a dance floor. Liquor can be consumed in the gaming area, though drinkers tend to hang out in the bar, which is a cavernous but compelling place, complete with cheap paneling, pool tables, and a huge projection screen TV. The tavern offers a daily dinner special, including a big fish or meat supper on Wednesdays. Otherwise, the menu includes the usual grill items. And, of course, there's the chance to bowl on one of eight lanes.

Overnight: The Old Rittenhouse Inn offers spectacular gourmet meals and the chance to sleep in a Queen Anne mansion, $99–$189 (715-779-5111). Bayfield on the Lake, $75–$165, and the Reiten Boatyard Condominium Hotel, $65–$95, offer the most spectacular views of the lake (715-779-3621 or 800-842-1199 for either hotel). For the budget-minded, the Bay Villa Motel, $26–$84, comes highly recommended (715-779-3252).

Other Reasons to Be Here: All attention centers on Lake Superior. Fishing and sailing are prime attractions, and Bayfield has many businesses that cater to these obsessions. The Bayfield Sailboat Race usually takes place the first week in July. The Big Top Chautauqua runs from June through August, including concerts, plays and historical musicals. In winter, consider driving Wisconsin's only state-maintained ice highway (Highway 13-Extension) from Bayfield to Madeline Island, the largest of the Apostle Islands. If you're driving across the chilly stretch on a weekend, it's likely that you'll be diverted by auto ice racing, one of Bayfield's most popular winter sports.

Lac Courte Oreilles Casino

Hayward, Wisconsin
800-422-2175
715-634-5643

Getting There: From Hayward, take Highway 27 to County Road B. The casino is at the intersection of County B and K, about four miles east of Hayward.

First Impression: All this and a big muskie, too.

Overview: Hayward is the kind of place many people think of when they use the expression "the lake up north." This is especially true for fishermen, though family resort traffic is heavy here from May through September. In February, international attention (particularly from Norway) focuses here on the American Birkebeiner cross-country ski race. But if there's anything that endears Hayward to visitors, it's the giant concrete muskie that looms above the Fishing Hall of Fame. Anybody visiting the casino—which, by the way, is pronounced "La-Coo-Tow-Ray"—will pass by the big, open-jawed fish. Stop, go inside and stand between the teeth. Nearest city: Duluth, Minn, 65 miles.

The Casino: Lac Courte Oreilles Casino is an $8 million, 35,000-square-foot facility that opened in the summer of 1993. It's a long, rectangular building that has a neat, orderly atmosphere and a dark, den-like feel. Its most striking feature is a long mural along one side of the interior that depicts the lifestyle of the Lake Superior Anishinabe through four seasons. The Lac Courte Oreilles Chippewa opened their first casino in the Hayward area in 1989, and they know that their business fluctuates like the fishing season. They have a cautious, conservative outlook that's reflected in the cool, deep-woods tone of the casino, where everything seems to be in its proper place.

Hours: 9 A.M. to 4 A.M. daily. Longer hours in summer.

In Play: 400 slot and video games (video poker, keno), nickel to $1 machines. 12 blackjack tables ($3–$200), using eight-deck shoes (three splits permitted; double-downs allowed except when splitting aces, which requires one additional card). Attached 300-seat bingo hall with evening sessions every day and afternoon matinees on Saturdays and Sundays.

Specials: Blackjack and bingo tournaments on "slow days." Call casino for details.

Amenities: Snack bar and ice cream shop. Buffet serves from 9 A.M. to midnight ($2.99, $4.99, $6.99) with seafood dinner on Wednesdays ($8.99). Gift shop specializes in Native American arts and crafts. No liquor.

Overnight: Casino employees recommend the Northern Pine International Inn, $43–$99 (800-777-7996), and the Cedar Inn Motel, $42–$105 (715-634-5332). Hayward has a huge variety of resorts and lodges, including the Northland Lodge, $43–$99, which features vacation log homes (715-462-3379), and Musky Joe's Twin Pines Resort, $75–$135 (715-462-3343). Some other lodging: Edelweiss Motel, $35–$49, (715-634-4679); Hayward Super 8, $35–$65 (800-800-8000); Riverside Motel, $36–$69 (715-634-2661).

Other Reasons to Be Here: The Muskie Festival is held here in June and the Honor the Earth Pow Wow in July attracts thousands of visitors. Lumberjack World Championships also take place in July. The Chequamegon Fat Tire Bike Race is in September and the American Birkebeiner ski race is in February. In summer, Hayward is a haven of activity: water skiing, fishing, hiking and, especially, golf. If you're brave enough to try for the big one, the Musky Inc. Fishing Tournament takes place in October. Bring heavy line.

Lake of the Torches Casino

Lac du Flambeau, Wisconsin
800-258-6724

Getting There: 11 miles west of Woodruff on Highway 47. The casino is in the center of the community's business district.

First Impression: A gambling den for the bus crowd.

Overview: Lac du Flambeau is an Ojibwe community of about 2,000 that lies in the center of one of Wisconsin's largest Indian reservations. The community is defined by a complex of meandering, frequently interconnected lakes—as is the entire reservation. Michigan's Upper Peninsula is less than 30 miles away. Nearest city: Rhinelander, about 40 miles southeast.

The Casino: The big rectangular building in the center of town is sheathed in knotty pine, very handsome and rustic. Inside, however, it's something of a disappointment, looking like a gambling K mart with a bad air-filtration system. A big "sports bar" anchors one side of the rectangle, and Mary's Kitchen, a fast-food snack bar with a little knot of booths, is on the other side. The casino caters heavily to tour operators, with a group of token-taking slots reserved for the bus crowd. Keno and low-pay video poker are popular, along with slots. The blackjack tables convert to $1 minimums on Mondays.

Hours: 24 daily.

In Play: 400 slot and video games (video poker, keno), nickel to $1. 14 blackjack tables ($3–$200), using four-deck shoes. Bingo sessions in a separate building.

Specials: $1 blackjack on Mondays. Free blackjack tournaments Tuesday afternoons. Daily bingo sessions in the nearby building include $600–$1,000 pots on Sundays and mini-jackpots every session except Friday matinees.

Amenities: Full bar offering cheap $1.25 drinks and frothy specialties. Mary's Kitchen specializes in grill and deep-fried foods.

Overnight: Resorts in Lac du Flambeau include Fence Lake Lodge, $50–$80, (715-588-3255) and Dillman's Sand Lake Lodge, $63–$381 seasonal (715-588-3143). Minocqua, located about 15 miles east on Highway 51, has a huge assortment of lodgings, from the top-rated Pines Motel, $39–$75 (715-356-5228), and the Pointe Hotel & Conference Center, $49–$159 (715-356-4431), to the Aqua Aire Motel, $25–$59 (715-356-3433), and a Super 8 Motel (715-356-9541).

Other Reasons to Be Here: This is a land of fishing. A hatchery and trout pond are located nearby, and there are several campgrounds in the area. In winter, snowmobiles sometimes outnumber cars. Casino personnel are happy to provide advice about other things to do, and you can call the Minocqua Chamber of Commerce (715-356-5266) to get a formal pitch and brochures.

Majestic Pines Casino

Black River Falls, Wisconsin
715-284-9098
800-657-4621

Getting There: Four miles east of Interstate 94 (Exit 116) on Highway 54.

First Impression: Just a slot shop.

Overview: Black River Falls is in the heart of Wisconsin's leafy countryside. There's a state park here, and it's a short hop to the strange House on the Rock and the American Players Theatre in Spring Green.

The Casino: Wisconsin gaming agreements allow each tribe to operate two casinos, plus bingo parlors. The Wisconsin Winnebago Nation, which also owns two first-class casinos in the state, stretched the definition by adding a slot parlor to its bingo hall near Black River Falls. What they've got is a small place for low-stakes gamblers. It's a cozy warren of rooms, often crowded.

The Winnebagos embarked on an ambitious expansion program in 1993, building two new casinos in Wisconsin. An expansion of the Black River Falls casino was under consideration, but it hinged on the success of the other new casinos. Planned for Majestic Pines: more slots.

Hours: 9 A.M. to 1 A.M. Sundays through Thursdays, 9 A.M. to 3 A.M. Fridays and Saturdays.

In Play: 210 slot and video games (video poker, keno and blackjack), nickel to $1. Bingo hall open evenings except Wednesdays, with matinees on Sundays. No blackjack tables.

Amenities: Small snack bar serving grill food. No liquor.

Overnight: The Best Western Arrowhead Lodge has 27 suites and 79 rooms, $39–$130, and offers an array of golf, entertainment and casino packages. Its restaurant and lounge features weekend entertainment (800-284-9471). The American Budget Inn, $37–$72, also features entertainment packages (715-284-4333 or 800-356-8018). Other lodging: The Pines Motor Inn, $30–$40, a full-service resort motel (715-284-5311 or 800-345-PINE).

Menominee Casinos

Keshena, Wisconsin
800-343-7778
715-799-4628

Getting There: In Keshena. Take Highway 29 north from Green Bay to Shawano, then Highway 47-55 north 7 miles to Keshena.

First Impression: A resort casino way up here?

Overview: The Menominees defied state authorities when they opened Wisconsin's first Indian casino here in 1988. The big complex now includes a 96-room hotel, an enormous tunnel-like bingo hall/slot shop called The Crystal Palace, and the big main casino, which was once called the Menominee Nation Casino. Keshena is on the frequently wild-running Wolf River, where summer rafting is a major attraction. Farther north, Highway 55 meanders through deep forests, marked by several river falls. Nearest city: Green Bay, 40 miles.

The Casino: Lots of players come here for the nickel slots and to enjoy the sunken show bar, which has entertainment every night except Mondays, plus Wednesday afternoons. On the other side of the parking lot, the former Crystal Palace appears to be the destination for the casino's older slot machines, and it has the ambiance of a bowling alley. The gaming venues are tacked-together buildings, with lots of odd-shaped spaces. But the overall effect is of a major casino operation, with room to stretch. The main casino offers lots of video games, including a whole room devoted to video poker, plus video keno, video blackjack and a small paper-keno playing area. The new hotel complex, built in 1994, includes a 250-seat buffet restaurant and the casino's smoke and gift shops, plus a video arcade.

Hours: 8 A.M. to 2 A.M. weekdays; 24 hours Fridays and Saturdays.

In Play: 680 slot and video games (video poker, keno, blackjack), nickel to $5 machines. 24 blackjack tables ($2–$100) using four-deck shoes (four splits allowed, with double-downs permitted after splits, except one card after splitting aces; dealer hits on soft 17s). Paper keno area. Bingo offered in 10 sessions per week, including every night, plus Tuesdays, Thursday and Saturday matinees (call 715-799-4495 for information).

Specials: Blackjack tournaments Monday and Thursday nights, with $10 buy-ins on Mondays and $15 buy-ins on Thursdays; all money returned in prizes. Free card club: The Menominee Valuable Player Club (MVP). Frequent coupon specials.

Amenities: Snack bar in casino. Buffet restaurant in hotel complex. Live entertainment nightly except Mondays, plus Wednesday afternoons. Liquor served in main casino, but prohibited in bingo hall.

Overnight: Hotel includes whirlpool suites, a swimming pool, gift shop, arcade, and smoke shop.

Other Reasons to Be Here: Wolf River rafting is a major attraction in summer. The tribe hosts a major pow wow in August. Fishing on Legend Lake is open to anyone with a Wisconsin license; all other reservation waters are reserved for tribal members.

Mohican North Star Casino & Bingo

Bowler, Wisconsin
715-787-3110
800-952-0195

Getting There: North of Highway 29 on County Road A, almost midway between Bowler and Gresham. Larger map: midway between Wittenberg and Shawano. Even larger map: midway between Wausau and Green Bay.

First Impression: Mom and Pop play here.

Overview: The Mohican North Star Casino has been wildly successful in attracting the bourgeoisie—which, by the way, is most of us. Nonetheless, the casino can be tough to find: in a grove of trees on a county road that meanders through Wisconsin countryside. The casino is a metal-sided building with brick trim. New additions in 1994 will almost double its size, though the future of the project has been clouded by disputes within the tribal management. Nearest city: Green Bay, about 60 miles east.

The Casino: This is a brightly lit place with an emporium feeling that includes high ceilings, wood trim on the soffits, lots of blinking signs and a neighborly staff. The low-end gambler comes here. Dollar blackjack is still offered on slow days. In 1994, construction began on an expansion to add about 250 slot machines and a dozen blackjack tables, plus a bar and lounge. A hotel is planned in 1995.

Hours: 10 A.M. to 2 A.M. Mondays through Wednesdays; 24 hours Thursdays through Sundays.

In Play: Between 368 slot and video games (video poker, keno), nickel to $1 machines. 12 blackjack tables ($1–$200), using two-deck pitch or five-deck shoes (four splits allowed and double-downs accepted after splits with exception of one-card on split aces; dealer hits on soft 17s). Daily bingo, except Tuesdays and Thursdays, in attached 350-seat hall. Expansions in 1994-95 will increase totals to 600 slot machines and 24 blackjack tables.

Specials: Blackjack tournaments planned. Card club offering merchandise and vacation trips. Frequent promotional coupons.

Amenities: Liquor served in gaming area at one price ($1.50) for any libation. Snack bar has enclosed glass eating area and serves a variety of grill food, plus daily specials. Entertainment in bingo hall on special weekends. Outdoor pig roasts and other activities during the summer.

Overnight: Nearest motels are in Shawano, including full-service resort lodging at the Best Western Village Haus Motor Lodge, $44–$85, (800-553-4479), and Cecil Fireside Inn, $35–$199 (715-745-6444). Other lodging in Shawano: Super 8 Motel, $36–$75 (800-800-8000); Pine Acre Motel (800-788-6665) and Siesta Villa Motel, $18–$50 (715-524-2108).

Other Reasons to Be Here: The International Sled Dog Racing Association uses the casino as its headquarters for a major race in February; the 1994 race attracted more than 100 teams. The Mohicans also own a golf course, located about five miles from the casino; casino/golfing specials are available. This is a popular hunting area in season. And, of course, there's always fishing.

Mole Lake Casinos

Mole Lake, Wisconsin
800-236-9466
715-478-5290 or 478-5565

Getting There: Seven miles south of Crandon on Highway 55. Mole Lake is an unincorporated community with one motel and no post office.

First Impression: No curb appeal, but surprisingly pleasant.

Overview: Mole Lake is a desolate community that lies on the edge of the Nicollet National Forest. Getting there is a chore, though you drive through some lovely woodlands and near many hidden lakes. After visiting the casinos, however, there's little reason to stay in Mole Lake. Nearest city: Rhinelander, 40 miles northwest.

The Casino: Technically, there are two casinos in Mole Lake, located across the highway from each other. The Grand Royale, on the west side of the road, has the least to offer. It's a small, square room, with a corner bar at one end and a single change booth on the other side. Most of the room is taken up by slots and low-paying poker machines. Posted over the blackjack tables are rules for two- and four-deck games. You're allowed to touch your cards with one hand if you're playing a two-deck pitch game, though the dealer can hit on a soft 17. If you decide to skip a hand, you have to sit out the rest of the shoe.

The Regency Resort Casino on the east side of the highway is a larger and more inviting place. From the outside, it doesn't look like much, but inside the layout draws you through a series of pleasant-sized rooms. There's more here than you might expect, including a small show room with a stage and dance floor, plus a bar. The bingo hall, with its cafeteria, is reached by walking through a small corridor to a connecting building.

Hours: 10 A.M. to 1 A.M. Sundays through Thursdays, 10 A.M. to 3 A.M. Fridays and Saturdays.

In Play: 480 slot and video games (video poker, keno), nickel to $1. 24 blackjack tables ($5–$100), using four-deck shoes, plus two-deck pitch games (check local rules before playing). Bingo every day except Wednesdays and Thursdays; call 715-478-2604 for information.

Amenities: Entertainment four nights a week, with live bands on Fridays and Saturdays. Liquor served throughout the casino. Snack bar at Grand Royale; snack bar and cafeteria at Regency Resort.

Overnight: The nearest motel is the bare-bones, though new, Mole Lake Motel (715-478-5770). Accommodations in Crandon include the Four Seasons Motel, $30–$50 (715-478-3377 or 800-341-8000), and the Pines Motel, $30–$59 (715-854-7987). The many resorts include the top-rated Glen Park Resort on Lake Metonga, $30–$100 summer only (715-478-3525), and Paust's Woods Lake Resort in Crivitz, $39–$65 (715-757-3722).

Other Reasons to Be Here: This is a haven for outdoor activity, particularly of the deep-woods-and-lakes variety. For more information contact the Crivitz Recreation Association, 715-757-3651.

Northern Lights Casino
Potawatomi Bingo

Wabeno, Wisconsin
800-487-9522

Getting There: South of Wabeno on Highway 32.

First Impression: Proudly serves cranberry juice on tap.

Overview: Wabeno and Carter are two villages in a region defined by the Nicollet National Forest. The area is covered with family- and fishing-oriented resorts and there are attractions like the Lumberjack Special, an old train that carries visitors to a nineteenth-century pioneer town, where they watch woodcarvers and blacksmiths. The casino/bingo hall is out in the countryside, atop a hill near Highway 32. The adjacent hotel opened in the summer of 1994. Nearest city: Green Bay, 85 miles southeast.

The Casino: The long, metal-covered building is faced with knotty pine siding and has separate entrances for casino and bingo players. Inside, it's an airy, few-frills gambling hall with an elevated sports bar in the back. Between the casino and bingo hall is a narrow, corridor-like room filled with four long rows of slot machines—probably a hellish place on busy days. There's an unusual emphasis on video poker here, the machines ranging from very tight to generous "8/5" nickel machines. Sandwiches can be purchased at the bar, and there's an institutional-like cafeteria in the bingo hall. A fine-dining restaurant can be found in the adjacent hotel which also has a swimming pool.

Hours: Opens 11 A.M. Mondays through Fridays, 10 A.M. Fridays and Saturdays. Closes after "everybody leaves." Earlier opening hours are sometimes posted in the summer.

In Play: 420 slot and video games (video poker, keno), nickel to $1 machines; 13 blackjack tables ($2–$200), using four-deck shoes (four splits allowed, with double downs after splits except for aces, which take one additional card); 450-seat bingo hall offers Wednesday through Sunday evening sessions and matinees in summer.

Amenities: Cafeteria meals daily, plus sandwiches at the bar. Liquor served in gaming area. Gift shop. Adjacent hotel.

Overnight: Hotel features 60 rooms, four of them suites, plus a pool and restaurant. Rates vary. Other lodging: The Waubee Lodge Resort, Motel & Supper Club, $35–$75, in Lakewood has all the amenities, including golf (800-492-8233); the North Star Motel, $34–$80 (800-326-6351).

Other Reasons to Be Here: The Brush Run 101 mud races are held in Crandon (about 30 miles from the casino) in June and over the Labor Day weekend. The Logging Museum near Wabeno features an antique train, the Lumberjack Special, that hauls visitors to a historic town near Laona.

Oneida Bingo & Casino

Green Bay, Wisconsin
800-238-4263
414-494-4500

Getting There: In Green Bay, across from the Austin Straubel Airport. Exit Interstate 43 on Highway 172 to reach the casino and hotel complex.

First Impression: Wisconsin's biggest—by far.

Overview: It's no surprise that the Oneida Casino looks a lot like a huge convention center, with a big, six-tier parking ramp and a hotel. If the gambling industry ever takes a nose dive, emergency plans call for the huge Oneida facility to switch to providing space for home shows and salesmanship meetings. To understand the casino complex, you have to adjust your terminology: There's the "new" casino, which is a huge hall with an attached parking ramp, the "new-old" casino, which is a huge addition to the former casino, just down the lane. And there's the "old casino," which is a series of smaller gaming areas. And while we're at it, there's also the slot-machine area of the Radisson Hotel, which operates in conjunction with the casino and can be reached on an enclosed walkway.

The Casino: It's enormous, but more awe-inspiring for its huge size rather than its contents. Starting with the "new" casino, one finds a big Las Vegas–style auditorium with a recessed, twinkle-light ceiling that depicts the Milky Way. The new casino has an upscale deli and pastry shop. A medium-priced restaurant, the Three Sisters, opened in 1994 with the completion of an adjacent convention facility. The new casino is attached to a 300-room Radisson Hotel, an upscale inn with its own pool, entertainment lounge (Purcell's) and pricey restaurant called The Shenandoah. From there, you can either walk or take a shuttle bus to the "new-old" or "old" casino buildings, which probably have the largest gaming areas in the complex. The biggest section is the "new-old" casino, which has its own cafeteria-style dining area.

A casino this size serves to emphasize the limitations on legal casino games in Wisconsin and some other states. Stroll about and all you see are slots, slots, slots, video poker, keno machines and scores of blackjack tables. There's not a lot of variety, only replication.

Hours: 24 daily. Blackjack played between 10 A.M. and 4 A.M.

In Play: More than 2,500 slot and video games (video poker, keno), nickel to $5 machines. 84 blackjack tables ($2–$200), using five-deck shoes and some two-deck shoes (three splits allowed at five-deck tables, one at two-deck tables; no double downs after splits on two-deck tables; dealers hit on soft 17s; splitting aces requires one additional card). 1,000-seat bingo hall offering morning, afternoon and evening sessions daily, plus "night-owl" sessions on weekends.

Specials: Blackjack tournaments twice each month on Tuesdays. Frequent coupon promotions.

Amenities: Free ramp parking. Wide selection of restaurants and snack bars. No liquor, though the hotel has a bar. No-smoking areas in the old casino. Shuttle bus service between gaming and hotel facilities. Gift shop. Entertainment nightly in Purcell's Lounge at the Radisson.

Overnight: The Radisson Inn, $73–$175, has 300 rooms, including 30 suites, plus a pool, sauna, an entertainment lounge and a fine-dining restaurant (800-333-3333). Other lodging: Holiday Inn City Centre, $66–$76 (800-457-2929; Budgetel Inn, $45–$53 (800-428-3438); Best Western Midway, $57–$72 (800-528-1234); Arena Motel, $28–$48 (414-494-5636).

Other Reasons to Be Here: The Green Bay Packers Hall of Fame is a must for gridiron fans, along with a tour of famous Lambeau Field. There's also the Bay Beach Amusement Park, which is famous for its low ride prices. The NEW Zoo, located in the 1,600-acre Brown County Reforestation Camp, is close to the National Railroad Museum and the Heritage Hill Living History Museum. For more information, call the city's visitor center at 800-236-2073.

Potawatomi Bingo

Milwaukee, Wisconsin
800-755-6171
414-645-6888

Getting There: 1721 West Canal, Milwaukee. The bingo and slot hall is in an industrial area along the Menomonee River, not far from Marquette University. Call the toll-free number from a touch-tone telephone and jot down the complicated directions.

First Impression: Biggest bingo-land in the Midwest.

Overview: Wisconsin gaming officials and Potawatomi tribal authorities have disagreed about the status of the "casino" that opened in Milwaukee in 1991. The tribe insists it isn't operating a casino, but a bingo parlor. A similar claim has been made by the Wisconsin Winnebago Nation about its Majestic Pines slot house and bingo hall near Black River Falls. Both places do not offer table games.

The Casino: From the vast parking lot, it looks like the Wisconsin casino prototype: a big, new metal-sided building. In this case, the colors are green and red. Inside, however, you discover an Olympic-size bingo hall. Two corridors at the front of the building have been tightly packed with about 200 reel-type slot machines and video poker games. The building also has three video rooms that have ticket-issuing machines. Nothing fancy here. But if you're really into big-buck bingo, this is the place to go.

Hours: 8 A.M. to 3 A.M. daily.

In Play: More than 200 slots and video games, mostly $1 machines.

Specials: An endless menu of bingo specials, with big jackpots.

Amenities: Snack bar. No liquor.

Overnight: Several Milwaukee hotels offer bingo specials, including the Quality Inn/Milwaukee West (414-771-4400) and the Airport Holiday Inn (414-764-1500).

Other Reasons to Be Here: Milwaukee has many of the attractions you would expect to find in a big city, including the Milwaukee County Zoo, Public Museum, and Broadway Theatre Center. Brewers baseball, the Milwaukee 150 Indy race, and soccer are the city's major sport enthusiasms. Milwaukee also has a national reputation for German, Serbian and Italian cuisine and a plentiful supply of sidewalk cafes and fancy bistros. If you're of a mind, try a gondola ride on the canal.

Rainbow Casino

Nekoosa, Wisconsin
715-886-4560
800-782-4560

Getting There: Four miles south of Nekoosa on County Trunk G. From Wisconsin Rapids, take Highway 34 south to Nekoosa before picking up the county road. Be prepared to stop and ask for directions in Nekoosa; it's easy to get lost.

First Impression: Did Frank Lloyd Wright design the restaurant?

Overview: The Wisconsin River has its charms, but this section is dominated by paper mills and industrial development. The locals tend to be self-effacing. Ask about things to do, and they usually crack a rueful smile, overlooking the scenic elements of the river and the outdoor recreational opportunities (golf, swimming, fishing, hunting). They're used to what they've got and not acquainted with tourist-oriented boosterism. This is middle America, though the new Rainbow Casino, which held its grand opening early in 1994, is changing that image. Local hotels and restaurants are noticing the casino trade; bus tours are more frequent; visitor traffic is picking up. Nearest city: Wisconsin Rapids, 10 miles north.

The Casino: The Wisconsin Winnebago Nation, which also operates the Ho-Chunk Casino at Lake Delton, spent less than $9 million to build the Rainbow Casino, but they got a lot for their money. At 37,000 square feet, it's a medium-sized facility, but feels a lot bigger because it's laid out in a large rectangular hall, with a sunken pit at the center beneath a high, stepped-up ceiling. Progressive slot machines, with gaudy lighted displays, dominate the floor. It's a loud place, but you can escape the babble by visiting the two restaurants. The upscale Rainbow Grille has a dandy, wood-trimmed bar and a secluded dining room that is easily the nicest casino dining spot in Wisconsin. It was designed by a Prairie School architect who centered attention on a massive stone fireplace and tall windows that face a pristine-feeling wooded grove.

Hours: 24 daily.

In Play: 600 slot and video games (video poker), nickel to $1, including many progressives; 24 blackjack tables ($3–$200), including two in a "high stakes" area, using six-deck shoes (splitting aces requires one additional card, double-downs allowed after splits). Bingo offered daily in a nearby building that once housed the old casino. Call 715-886-3222 for bingo schedules.

Specials: Major seven-week blackjack tournaments. Call the toll telephone number for additional tournaments and specials.

Amenities: The nicest-looking restaurant of any Wisconsin casino, offering steaks and seafood at prices that range from $8 to $17 for dinner, $4 to $8 for lunch. Prime rib specials on Tuesdays and Thursdays. Full bar, though liquor is not allowed in the gaming area. Snack bar offers fast grill food and sandwiches and has a private eating area.

Overnight: There are no nearby motels and, in fact, very few nearby buildings. The Mead Inn in Wisconsin Rapids is universally acknowledged as the best lodge in the area, with its own pool, sauna, whirlpool, bar and upscale dining room, $45–$84 (800-THE MEAD). Other recommended lodging (in Wisconsin Rapids): Wilbern's Motel, $40–$60 (715-423-5506); The Chalet Motel and Restaurant, $34–$50 (715-423-7000); Camelot Motel, $25–$40 (715-325-5111).

Other Reasons to Be Here: Nearby Stevens Point has several attractions, including the Rainbow Falls Water Amusement Park and the SentryWorld Sports Center, with its magnificently manicured golf course. For the arts and crafts crowd, there's Herrschners Retail Outlet Store, home of the largest mail order craft catalog in the world. East of Wisconsin Rapids is the Amish village of Amherst. Quilt and consignment sales take place there throughout the summer, usually on weekends.

St. Croix Casino & Hotel

Turtle Lake, Wisconsin
800-846-8946

Getting There: On Highway 8 in Turtle Lake.

First Impression: Whose woods these are I think I know . . .

Overview: Turtle Lake is a nice little sportsman's village in Western Wisconsin. Fishing, hunting and snowmobiling are topics of local interest. The community feels remote, but it really isn't; the glitter of Minneapolis/St. Paul is just 80 miles away. For this reason, the St. Croix Casino attracts an urban crowd as well as tourists and locals. At the same time, it's something of a niche casino, relying on its smaller size and its unique appearance.

The Casino: This is, far and away, the strangest looking gambling establishment in Wisconsin. The interior is made to resemble a birch forest in the moonlight, with plaster trees, faux-stone columns and chairs that are trimmed with imitation beaver pelts and animal hides. Overhead, stars twinkle through birch leaves, and the blackjack tables are elevated under frames of fake birch logs. By big-city standards, the St. Croix is small, but it's got all the services—including two bars, one with nightly entertainment, plus a buffet room and a first-class restaurant. A major expansion in 1994 will provide convention facilities and additional slot machines.

Hours: 24 daily.

In Play: 700 slot and video games (video poker, keno), nickel to $5 machines. 32 blackjack tables ($3–$200) using six-deck shoes (splitting aces requires one additional card; double downs allowed after splits). The Indian Bay Bingo hall is 15 miles away.

Specials: Very busy blackjack tournaments on Tuesdays (100 percent payback, $30 buy-in). Joining the TLC Players Club qualifies for many discounts and special promotions, plus merchandise as playing premiums. The casino has several big jackpot progressives that sometimes climb to more than $20,000.

Amenities: The Buffalo Brothers Saloon, named for the casino's former management company, features nightly entertainment and free bar snacks. The bar is framed by a group of ghostly, glass windows that pulsate with blue light and show carved images of Indians, frontiersmen and animals important to Ojibwe culture. The Me-Ki-Noc Restaurant offers huge portions for prices that range from $3 for a sandwich to $13 for a dinner entree. The TLC Room offers daily buffets and is the venue for bands and stage shows on Fridays and Saturdays. The special $10.99 seafood buffet on Thursdays attracts a devoted crowd. At the other end of the casino, a portable hot-dog stand sells big, tasty wieners for $1.50, along with sandwiches and ice cream.

Overnight: The casino has its own hotel, located about a block away, with shuttle service provided. If you plan on staying there, join the TLC Players Club before you check in and qualify for a discount on rooms. The hotel is new, resembling a budget chain motel, but it has a hospitality room and continental breakfasts. Rates are $44–$59, though special rates are common (800-782-9987).

Other Reasons to Be Here: In addition to the twin Wisconsin obsessions (snowmobiling and fishing), the area has many county and state trails, some of them restricted to cross-country skiing or hiking. The Trollhagen Ski resort is 25 miles away, and two adjacent state parks—one in Wisconsin, one in Minnesota—are about 35 miles west, in the St. Croix River valley.

CHAPTER 8
PLAYING THE GAMES

The gambling industry in the Midwest is going through a period of explosive change. But one thing never changes: The odds at a casino are always against you.

Casinos are in the business of redistributing wealth: take from the many and give to the few, with a nice profit left over for the owners. There's no such thing as a non-profit casino. Going to a casino ought to viewed as entertainment—something you pay to do. Remember, in the long run, the only way to make money at a casino is to own one.

By employing a little skill and a lot of self-control, however, you can keep your casino entertainment costs within reason. With that goal in mind, this chapter includes brief explanations of most of the games played at casinos in the Midwest, along with some advice on how to play them.

A few general rules:

• Never risk more than you can afford to lose. Decide how much you're going to spend on your gambling expedition before you go to the casino and don't change your mind after you get there. If you need to avoid temptation by leaving your checkbook and credit cards at home, think seriously—very seriously—about staying away from casinos altogether.

• Wager in accordance with your bankroll. Some experts say you should never wager more than 1/40th of your total stake on a single bet. Others say you should plan on being able to cover at least 80 bets in any game you decide to play. In any case, if you plan to spend no more than $40 during your casino visit, it's probably not a good idea to start by sitting at a $5 blackjack table.

• Don't play games that you don't understand. Find out if there are beginner's tables for blackjack (many of the bigger casinos have them). If you own a personal computer, buy an inexpensive video-poker or blackjack program, one that signals mistakes in your play, and practice, practice, practice.

- Don't get drunk in a casino. Don't even try for that pleasant glow.
- When you're losing, don't chase your losses by increasing your wagers. If you're winning, don't fall into the trap of thinking that you're playing with the casino's money. It's not their money until you've lost it.
- Decide how much you're going to win. The saying "quit while you're ahead" was probably uttered by the world's first gambler after he left a pre-historic casino with an empty pouch. Some gamblers use the two-pouch method, placing winnings in one pocket and their gambling stake in another pocket, then never touching their winnings.
- Don't use money to make a good impression on the staff. Casino operators are in the hospitality business. It's not your job to entertain them; it's their job to entertain you. If they make you feel uncomfortable, leave.

Blackjack

The Object of the Game: Blackjack is played with one or more standard 52-card decks. An ace counts as 1 or 11, face cards count as 10 and all other cards, 2 through 10, count as their face value. The suits have no significance.

The object is to beat the dealer by accumulating cards that total as close as possible to 21 without "going bust" by exceeding 21. If your total beats the dealer, you're paid an amount equal to your bet.

At the start of the game, each player and the dealer receive two cards. A blackjack, or "natural," is an ace and a 10 or face card that are received in the opening deal. Unlike other winning hands, a blackjack pays 3 to 2.

You can split two cards of equal value by adding a wager that is equal to the first, then playing both hands separately. You can also "double down" by adding an amount equal to your first wager in exchange for one additional card.

In the casino, the dealers are "mechanicals." They make no decisions regarding their hands, but take a card, or "hit," when their cards total 16 or less. They "stand" (in most cases) when their cards total 17 or more.

Blackjack, Midwestern Style: Blackjack is the most popular table game in American casinos, and the Midwest is no exception. Virtually every casino offers the standard "face-up" version of the game where players never touch their cards and dealers use a "shoe" that holds two to eight decks from which hands are dealt. Some casinos offer fewer decks at higher-minimum tables and a few quietly offer hand-held "pitch" games, usually with two decks. As the industry ages, some casinos are offering variations on the game—such as "double exposure" blackjack, where both of the dealer's cards are dealt face up, and "multiple action" blackjack, where customers play one hand against as many as three hands played by the dealer.

The two Grand Casinos in Minnesota—at Hinckley and Mille Lacs—even have blackjack tables where players face a big TV dealer and receive their cards on individual monitors. The game can be played for as little as a quarter a hand, though most of the video tables require $1 minimums.

Playing Blackjack: If you've never played blackjack, you shouldn't try to master the game by reading a book. Many large casinos have beginner's tables, where the game is taught without wagering. During slow periods, when the dealers stand stoically with their cards fanned out across the table, you can ask to be shown how to play (you may have to bet, however). If they don't smile cheerfully while they show you how, you're probably in the wrong casino.

Played with skill, blackjack offers the best odds of any game currently available in the Midwest. If you decide that it's your game, invest in some of the devices that pound the skills into your head: a computer program, if you own your own PC, or even one of the hand-held electronic games. Or practice at home with a friend.

Some casinos have slot-type blackjack games that you can play for as little as a quarter a hand. The machines electronically shuffle the cards for each hand and many have awful rules—such as keeping ties and not allowing double downs on any number except 11. But a beginner can practice on them.

Betting limits are always posted on the table. Beginners should select $2 or $3 tables, where the atmosphere is less tense and where mistakes are tolerated. The myth persists that bad blackjack players hurt other blackjack players. In reality, your hand is independent and, in the long run, will be unaffected by the way other players play the game.

Have the courage to seek out crowded tables. Crowded tables mean fewer hands per person per hour. You'll have more time to think, plus it's more fun and less costly.

Remember to tip the dealer. Many are working for minimum wage. During the course of the session, place a side bet next to your own bet before the cards are dealt and indicate that it's a tip. If you win, so does the dealer. If you lose, the money goes to the house.

Once you've learned the basics, you'll soon realize that insignificant-seeming rules can be very important. Even if you're not a "counter," you'll find that tables with fewer decks in the shoe allow you to get a sense of the way the game is going. It is to the player's advantage to have a bigger ratio of high cards (9s, 10s and aces) in the shoe. Conversely, it is to the casino's advantage to have more low cards (2–7) in the shoe.

Rules that favor the casino include limits on when you can double down and how often you can split hands. Ideally, you want to be able to double down as often as possible—even when it's a stupid thing to do. Casinos never allow you to double down after you've split aces, though they do require you to take one additional card.

Standard Blackjack Strategy

Your hand	Dealer's up card									
	2	3	4	5	6	7	8	9	10	A
9	H	D	D	D	D	H	H	H	H	H
10	D	D	D	D	D	D	D	D	H	H
11	D	D	D	D	D	D	D	D	D	H
12	H	H	S	S	S	H	H	H	H	H
13	S	S	S	S	S	H	H	H	H	H
14	S	S	S	S	S	H	H	H	H	H
15	S	S	S	S	S	H	H	H	H	H
16	S	S	S	S	S	H	H	H	H	H
A-2	H	H	H	D	D	H	H	H	H	H
A-3	H	H	H	D	D	H	H	H	H	H
A-4	H	H	D	D	D	H	H	H	H	H
A-5	H	H	D	D	D	H	H	H	H	H
A-6	H	D	D	D	D	H	H	H	H	H
A-7	S	D	D	D	D	S	S	H	H	H
2-2	H	SP	SP	SP	SP	SP	H	H	H	H
3-3	H	SP	SP	SP	SP	SP	H	H	H	H
6-6	SP	SP	SP	SP	SP	H	H	H	H	H
7-7	SP	SP	SP	SP	SP	SP	H	H	H	H
8-8	SP	SP	SP	SP	SP	SP	SP	SP	SP	SP
9-9	SP	SP	SP	SP	SP	S	SP	SP	S	S
10- 10	S	S	S	S	S	S	S	S	S	S
A-A	SP	SP	SP	SP	SP	SP	SP	SP	SP	SP

D = Double down
H = Hit
S = Stand
SP = Split
■ Always stand on 17-21
■ Never split 4s or 5s

The most common variation that favors the casino is a rule that allows dealers to hit on "soft 17s" (an ace plus other cards adding up to 6). You want to find a table where the dealer stands on all 17s. If the casino posts a rule saying that the house wins all ties, it's a fleecing factory.

Basic Blackjack Strategy: If you talk to anyone about blackjack, you'll hear the expression "basic strategy" or "playing the basics" again and again. In theory, playing basic strategy in a casino that has favorable blackjack rules reduces the house advantage to 1 percent or less. But the fact is, the average person never masters basic strategy well enough to consistently beat the house.

Complete charts for basic strategy are available everywhere (including in this guide), and most are identical. You can, however, play a fairly competent game of blackjack by understanding eight general rules:

1. Double 10 and 11 when the dealer's up card is 2 through 9.
2. Stand if you hold 12 to 16 and the dealer's up card is 2 through 6.
3. Hit if you hold 12 to 16 and the dealer's up card is 7 through a 10 card or an ace.
4. Stand if you hold 17 to 21, but always hit on a soft 17.
5. Double down if you hold 9 and the dealer's up card is 3 through 6.
6. Always split 8s and aces.
7. Never split 5s or 10 cards.
8. Never take insurance.

These rules cover most of the combinations in blackjack. There are some additional tips for playing "soft hands," where you receive an ace (which counts as 1 or 11) and an additional card:

1. Hit if you hold an ace and 2 or 3. Double down if the dealer's up card is a 5 or 6.
2. Hit if you hold an ace and 4 or 5. Double down if the dealer's up card is 4 through 6.
3. Hit if you hold an ace and a 6. Double down if the dealer's up card is 3 through 6.
4. Stand if you hold an ace and a 8 or 9.

If you are dealt an ace and a seven, for a total of 18, you have the most complicated hand in blackjack. The conventional wisdom is you should stand on 18s. If you're more adventuresome, however, here are some suggestions:

1. Stand if the dealer's up card is a 2, 7 or 8.
2. Double down if the dealer's up card is 3 through 6.
3. Hit if the dealer's up card is a 9, 10-card, or ace.

For more advice on playing blackjack, including how-to books on card counting, go to a bookstore and check the section on games. Highly recommended: *The World's Greatest Blackjack Book* by Lance Humble and Carl Cooper.

Blackjack Variations: A few Midwest casinos are starting to offer "Double Exposure" blackjack, where both of the dealer's cards are dealt face up. In exchange for being able to see the hole card, the casino imposes limits on doubling down and sometimes takes all ties. As a result, the strategy for playing double exposure is vastly different from standard blackjack.

Another, more popular variant, is "Multiple Action Blackjack," which was first developed several years ago in Las Vegas. The player wagers up to three bets on spots that are arranged vertically in from of each betting position. The cards are dealt in the usual manner, except the dealer doesn't take a hole card. The player plays his hand, making decisions based on the dealer's up card.

Assuming the player doesn't bust, the dealer plays his first hand according to the rules and the player wins or loses his first hand. The dealer then discards all but his original up card and plays another round against the player's original hand and his second bet. After that, the dealer plays a third round against the player's hand and his third wager.

The variation allows the house to speed up the game, booking more bets and more action in a shorter amount of time. It also encourages players to stand with weak totals (12-16) because going bust means the player loses all three wagers instead of one. If you play this game, you should use standard blackjack strategy and learn to gulp quietly when you go bust and lose three wagers.

Some casinos also have introduced side bets—such as betting that the player's first two cards will total more or less than 13. These silly bets are separate from the standard blackjack wagers.

Slot Machines

Slot machines are the leading revenue producers in any casino. For the consumer, they have the same characteristics as the lottery: they're easy to play, they offer the possibility of a big jackpot payoff, and they're a great equalizer. Everybody is equal in a slot-machine parlor—and for many, that's a comforting fact.

But here's another fact: In the long run, you cannot beat slot machines. They are computers, programmed to pay out a certain percentage of the money put into them. At first glance, that percentage appears to be high, usually averaging between 89 and 94 percent among all the machines in a typical Midwest casino.

But over the long haul, a "hold" of less than 10 percent grinds away at your bankroll until it's gone. Yes, the sound of winners squealing with delight is very common in a slot parlor. But they usually keep playing, and when it's time to go home, they leave with less money than they had when they arrived.

Hopefully, they had a good time. Some people, in fact, are even soothed by the trance-like, Pavlovian mental state that the games can induce. If you're not entertained by slot machines, you shouldn't play them.

Slot machines come in two basic styles. With the exception of Minnesota, the majority of slot machines in Midwest casinos are modern versions of the three-reel mechanical machines that were invented nearly a century ago. Minnesota is unique because it allows only video machines, though most produce a TV version of the three-reel mechanicals that are found in other states. In Minnesota, however, you will also find a wide variety of multi-screen machines that have more playing options.

In deciding which slot machine to play, and how to play it, you have to choose between risk and reward. Nickel machines, which require a less risky portion of your bankroll to play, also provide the worst reward—sometimes averaging as little as an 80 percent return. Higher-denomination machines are usually looser, but you also stand the chance of losing more money if you play them.

The same risk/reward thesis holds true for "progressive" machines. A progressive is a group of linked-together slots that are connected to a slowly increasing jackpot. Each player contributes a small percentage of potential winnings to the big prize and, eventually, somebody wins it—usually somebody else. Essentially, you risk more for the chance to win the big reward.

After you've become familiar with slot machines, you'll discover that some tend to pay off with infrequent, big rewards, while others dribble away, returning something with nearly every pull. It's a mistake to think that the dribblers are looser. In reality, one machine is aimed at the gambler who needs lots of reinforcement in the form of frequent paybacks, while the other appeals to the dogged player who is patiently seeking a big-prize cookie.

In general, however, machines with lower jackpots pay back smaller amounts more frequently. When you walk up to a slot machine, look at its prize schedule. For the same wager, one machine may pay a jackpot of 1,000 coins and the machine next to it may have a top prize of 20,000 coins. One has a bigger top prize, but the other is more likely to return smaller prizes.

Don't stake out a slot machine, waiting for it to become "due." The computer chips that determine slot winners give new meaning to the word random. In fact, the definition of an average payout of a slot machine is often stated in terms of millions of bets—something like 17 million pulls—over the life of the machine.

A few words about playing "max coins." The standard mantra in a slot parlor is "play max coins, play max coins, play max coins." The first piece of advice you'll hear from other slot players is that wagering the maximum number of coins in a slot machine—usually three to eight coins—increases the machine's payout percentage.

This is true—to a point. On most machines, a maximum bet is required to qualify for a jackpot. This increases the machine's theoretical payout by one or two percentage points, but it doesn't add anything to the payout percentage that the gambler receives unless it comes in the form of the jackpot.

However, it does simplify your risk/reward decision when it comes to deciding how many coins to wager on each pull. You either bet one coin (the smallest risk) or bet the maximum coins (the biggest reward). Anything in between—say, three coins on a five-coin machine—doesn't make sense.

One last thing: If the casino has a slot club, join it. A small portion of the money you lose will be recouped through club benefits.

Video Poker

For many non-table players in a casino, video poker is the game of choice. It is popular because many slot-machine players eventually decide that they want to exert some control over their gambling fate and they soon learn that video poker gives them a better edge than non-skill slot playing. The video version is significantly different from the friendly little poker game you played in your basement, and learning to play it correctly takes time and practice. But learning just a few skills can help improve your chances.

First, there's the significant task of choosing the right machine. Most beginners and bona fide video poker experts stick with the game that's identified as Draw Poker, Jacks or Better. This is the only game that will be discussed in this section. Other types of video poker include Deuces Wild, Joker Poker, Bonus Poker, Tens or Better and unique variations on each of these games. All are played with different strategies.

You can't tell the payback percentage on a slot machine, but you can discover the theoretical payback on a video poker game, if you know how to interpret the information printed on the machine. Here's how:

First, make sure it's a Draw Poker machine and that it returns your bet on a pair of jacks or better. The first column of the payout schedule for one-coin bets should also indicate that the machine returns two coins for two pair, three coins for three of a kind, and four coins for a straight. With one coin bet, the machine also should pay 25 coins for four of a kind, 50 coins for a straight flush and 250 coins for a royal flush.

Once this has been established, check to see what the machine pays for a flush and a full house. Then check the last column for the five-coin royal flush jackpot. If it isn't 4,000 coins or a progressive jackpot, don't play the machine. If it requires a sixth coin to qualify for the progressive jackpot, leave the casino.

The payouts for flush and full house are standard reference points for people who seek out the best machines. Low payback machines, sometimes called "Atlantic City machines," pay five coins for a flush and six coins for a full house when one coin is bet. In video-poker parlance, these are called 6/5 machines.

In Las Vegas, it's not hard to find a machine that pays six coins for a flush and nine coins for a full house. These are called 9/6 or "full pay" machines because, if played perfectly (without mistakes), a 9/6 machine will return about 99.5 percent of the money played through it on five-coin bets.

Unfortunately, about the best you can do in the Midwest is an 8/5 progressive machine (five coins for straight, eight coins for flush). With perfect play, the theoretical payback on an 8/5 non-progressive machine is 97.4 percent.

Unlike slots, there's no additional "hold" on a progressive poker machine—and this can work to your advantage. Theoretically, when the progressive jackpot on an 8/5 quarter machine reaches $2,200 for a royal flush, perfect play will make it a break-even gamble. For a dollar progressive, the jackpot would have to be $8,800.

This doesn't mean that your odds of getting a royal flush increase—actually, you have about one chance in 46,000 hands of cards. But the theoretical chance of staying even over the long haul is good enough to make the 8/5 progressive a good machine to select for a cheap, limited session of entertainment.

Most casinos in the Midwest attach 6/5 machines to progressives or require $5 a pop to make a maximum bet on a five-coin 8/5 machine. It's often hard to find a nickel video poker game that isn't a 6/5 machine, though 7/5 nickel machines (seven coins for a full house, five for a straight) turn up now and again.

One of the great exceptions is Bad River Casino in northern Wisconsin, which has a quarter 8/5 progressive in its main casino and rows of 8/5 nickel machines upstairs in a crowded little room.

After touring many of the casinos in the Midwest a few years ago, video-poker expert Lenny Frome suggested that gamblers protest the lack of 9/6 machines by limiting their play to single-coin quarter or nickel bets. In Minnesota, however, such protests would have to result in a major change in state-wide regulations, since 9/6 machines theoretically return more than the 98 percent payout limit allowed under gaming compacts.

Perfect Play: The term "perfect play" is used often to describe the strategy for playing video poker without mistakes. Books on video poker usually list charts with every possible combination of five cards that you might receive on the first draw, along with the correct decision you should make on holding and discarding. There are, however, some basic rules:

1. If your best hand is a pair—high or low—keep them and discard any unpaired high cards.

2. If you don't have a pair, keep any card above a 10 to a maximum of two, unless they are in the same suit. If you have two unsuited face cards and an ace, discard the ace and keep the face cards (this way, your odds increase of drawing to a straight). If two of your three high cards are suited, keep those two and discard the unsuited card.

3. Don't hold three cards in an effort to complete a straight or a flush.

4. Don't draw one card to an inside straight (you shouldn't try that in any form of poker). But do draw a single card to an open-ended straight (one that can be completed at either end).

5. If your dealt hand has no pair, no high card and no one-card draw to a flush or open-ended straight, it's garbage. Draw five new cards.

6. Don't hold "kicker" cards. This is a high card—a king, for example—that is often held with a pair of low cards. In table poker, it's sometimes useful to hold kickers in order to bluff. In video poker, it lessens your chances of drawing to three of a kind.

If you're interested in making video poker your game, there are dozens of books on the subject that can be purchased at bookstores or through gambling magazines. Some of the most respected authors are Stanford Wong, Lenny Frome, and Bradley Davis.

If you own a personal computer, there are plenty of low-cost, shareware and even free poker programs. The best include detailed play manuals and signal you when you've made a mistake. Some also run computer simulations of lengthy perfect play sessions of video poker. After running a few simulations, you'll discover that the difference between a winning session and losing lesson of video poker usually boils down to getting, or missing, one or two high-paying hands.

Other Games

Keno: There are two traditional keno parlors in Iowa—at the Mesquaki Casino in Tama and the WinnaVegas Casino in Sloan—that operate in the same low-key manner as ubiquitous keno outfits in Las Vegas. But video keno is very big in the Midwest, even though it has the distinction of being the casino game with the biggest house edge.

Parlor keno, a variant of bingo, is a leisurely game where the big house advantage is balanced against the slow per-hour rate of loss. At Mesquaki and WinnaVegas, keno runners take your tickets while you pay attention to other things—such as eating a sandwich, or doing your Chapter 11 bankruptcy paperwork. Both paper keno and video keno work the same way.

In video keno, you select up to 10 numbers between one and 80. Then the machine randomly selects 20 numbers and you are paid according to how many of your numbers matched, or "hit." The house edge is a whopping 20 percent.

People like keno because a small investment can produce really big prizes, though the odds of winning are terrible. At WinnaVegas, the top prize is $100,000.

Unfortunately, video keno maintains the huge house advantage, but allows the game to be played fast enough to wipe out a bankroll in a short period of time. Nonetheless, the game remains popular. The newer video machines are quite lively, with numbered balls racing across the screen during cycles of the game that last only a few seconds.

Craps: Craps is played on the riverboats in Iowa and Illinois and at the three Indian casinos in Iowa. The dice game is also legal in North Dakota, but it hasn't caught on there. Three Iowa boats—Sioux City Sue, the Clinton Riverboat Casino and The President in Davenport—offered quarter craps early in 1994. Craps is an exciting, complicated, visceral game. The riverboat and Iowa games use the standard Las Vegas layout, where the casino edge is a low 1.4 percent for the line bets (pass, don't pass, come and don't come). Most of the Illinois boats offer double odds on additional free-odds wagers. This reduces the casino advantage to 0.6 percent.

Some Minnesota casinos have a high-tech video version of the game called "crapless craps" that is played at a giant, six-station video table and has a house advantage on a pass line bet of 5.4 percent. For the beginner, these video versions are a good place to start, since a single bet can be as low as 25 cents.

In Minnesota, video craps was introduced at the Grand Casinos in Mille Lacs and Hinckley. The game also can be found at Mystic Lake Casino in Shakopee, at Treasure Island near Red Wing and at Jackpot Junction near Redwood Falls.

No amount of written instructions can prepare the player for the experience of a craps table, where the action is fast, furious, loud and often confusing. It's the traditional game for big bettors, where a lot of money changes hands in a short period of time.

If you plan to play, know what you're doing. Recommended reading: *Winning at Casino Craps*, by Edwin Siberstang (David McKay Co., $6.95 in paperback).

Roulette: This wonderfully pretty game is said to have been invented in the seventeenth century by Blaise Pascal, whose theories of probability also were used by Edward Thorpe when he devised his winning strategy for blackjack. The game is played in Iowa and Illinois casinos. All use the standard 38-pocket American wheel with the green "0" and "00" slots. The finest roulette setup can be found at WinnaVegas in Sloan, Iowa, which has a beautiful, double-sided table with a big wheel in the center. All other casinos use the compact little tables that are common everywhere.

Betting limits vary from casino to casino and are often different depending on the time of day—higher in the evening, low in the morning. Some Iowa casinos had 25-cent chips before the bet limits were repealed in 1994.

As any gambler will tell you, roulette gives the casino a high edge—5.26 percent—and it's played fast. You can get a revealing lesson about the fates of the game by watching a few spins. Chips are piled all over the place, the ball drops and the dealer rakes in just about everything.

You'll see a few people playing with paper and pencil. They're system players who refuse to believe that every drop of the ball is completely independent of every drop of the ball that ever happened—or ever will happen. Some will argue that no roulette wheel is perfectly balanced and that certain numbers will occur more often on certain wheels. Dream on.

Roulette is a simple game, but first-timers sometimes get confused by it. All you have to do is hand over some money and tell the dealer the value you want placed on the chips. The dealer will assign you a chip color, then take one chip from that color and place it on the edge of the wheel with a "Lammer" button on top of it to designate its value. If you're playing the minimum value chips, no Lammer is necessary.

The sign on the table indicates what minimum bets are on the "inside" (straight-up numbers and combinations) and the low-odds on the "outside" (red, black, odd, even, 1 to 18, 19 to 36, and the first, second, or third 12-number bets).

Here's a list of roulette bets and payoffs:

Single number. Also called "straight up." The easiest bet with the worst chance of winning. Pays 35 to 1.

Two numbers. The split bet. Put your chip on the line between two numbers. Pays 17 to 1.

Three numbers. The "street bet." Put your chip on the line at the bottom of a three-number line. Pays 11 to 1.

Four numbers. Put your chip at the crossed intersection that connects four numbers. Pays 8 to 1.

Five numbers. There's only one possible. Put your chip on the crossed line that separates "0" from "1" and the "1st 12" box. Pays 6 to 1.

Six numbers. Looks something like a street bet, except the chip is placed on the "T" intersection between two three-number lines and the outside bet boxes. Called the "double street" bet, it pays 5 to 1.

Even money bets. Red, black, odd or even numbers, 1 through 18 or 19 through 36.

2 to 1 bets. Easy to understand. You bet all the numbers in a particular horizontal line. Put your chip in the box marked "2 to 1."

When you're done, remember to cash in your chips at the table—if you have any left.

Mini-Baccarat: Mini-Baccarat is a compact version of traditional baccarat, but played at a smaller blackjack-like table with a single dealer.

When it opened in 1993, the Hollywood Riverboat Casino in Aurora, Ill., had a full-size baccarat table, with formal-clad dealers and a velvet rope to separate upscale players from the common rabble. But the table was removed when nobody showed up to play.

Only a few riverboats offer the mini-baccarat version. All charge the standard 5 percent commission for winning banker bets. The dealer keeps track of the commissions and players are expected to settle up before they leave.

Baccarat is an easy game to play, because the rules are rigid for the way the cards are dealt. You either bet on the house or on the player. Only dopes bet on ties, because the house's edge is a whopping 14 percent. Otherwise, the casino's advantage is slight, but insurmountable. With the commission, the house edge on a bank bet is 1.06 percent and it's 1.23 percent on a player bet. There is a card-counting strategy for baccarat, but many players simply concentrate on betting the bank.

The Big Six Wheel: The Big Six, or money wheel, can be found in a few Illinois and Iowa casinos and it was introduced in North Dakota in 1994, where it may replace a crude, roulette-like game called the Paddle Wheel.

The game is as simple as tossing your money into the wind. The wheel looks like the Wheel of Fortune from television, with 54 spots around the circumference that are decorated with currency of different denominations. You place your bet on a table decorated with identical bills, the wheel is spun and winners are paid—every now and then.

The name of the game comes from the six possible payoffs. Of the 54 spots, 24 pay even money; 15 spots pay 2 to 1; seven spots pay 5 to 1; four spots pay 10 to 1, two spots pay 20 to 1, and one spot pays 40 to 1.

The house advantage ranges from 11.1 percent to 24 percent. Many save their last dollar for a bet on the Big Six Wheel, and they usually get to play just once.

About the Author

   David Hawley writes a weekly column for the *Saint Paul Pioneer Press* about gambling in Minnesota and western Wisconsin. His columns encompass a range of topics—from slot machine play and payoff odds to the design and amenities of the casinos.
   He has been a newspaper reporter for 22 years, and his career includes a stint with the Associated Press and as music and drama critic for the *Pioneer Press*. He also has written two plays that have been produced.
   Hawley has followed the rapid growth of casinos in the Midwest, visiting them as they opened and taking a critical look at their facilities.
   He enjoys gambling—but only on an expense account.